ICECREAM

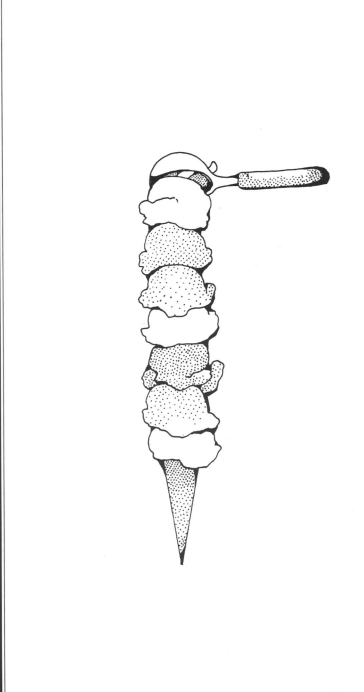

SIMPLE PLEASURES

ICECREAM

FOLCO PORTINARI

Webb & Bower

MICHAEL JOSEPH

The excerpt from *War and Peace* by Tolstoy on pages 86–7 is reproduced from the Penguin Classics edition, translation copyright 1957 Rosemary Edmonds.

The excerpt from 'Storm on Fifth Avenue' by Siegfried Sassoon at the beginning of Chapter VIII is reproduced by kind permission of George Sassoon.

First published in Great Britain in 1989 by
Webb & Bower (Publishers) Limited,
9 Colleton Crescent, Exeter, Devon EX2 4BY,
in association with Michael Joseph Limited,
27 Wright's Lane, London W8 5TZ

Penguin Books Ltd, Registered Offices: Harmondsworth,
Middlesex, England
Penguin Books Australia Ltd, Ringwood, Victoria, Australia
Penguin Books Canada Ltd, 2801 John Street, Markham, Ontario,
Canada L3R 1D4
Penguin Books (NZ) Ltd, 182–190 Wairau Road, Auckland 10, New Zealand

Designed by Carlotta Maderna / Vic Giolitto
Series Editor Mariarosa Schiaffino
Illustrations by Vittorio Salarolo / Il Collezionista / Civica Raccolta
Stampe Achille Bertarelli

Production by Nick Facer / Rob Kendrew

Translated from the Italian by Kerry Milis
Copyright © 1987 Idealibri SpA, Milan
Copyright © 1989 Idealibri SpA, Milan, for English translation

British Library Cataloguing in Publication Data

Portinari, Folco
Ice-creams.
1. Icecream
I. Title II. Series III. Voglia
di gelato. *English*
641.3'74

ISBN 0–86350–264–4

Typeset in Great Britain by Scribes, Exeter, Devon

Printed and bound in Italy by Grafiche Editoriali Ambrosiane di Milano

CONTENTS

MELTING WITH PLEASURE

LATELY, for reasons to do purely with age, I have been tempted to try to become (better late, than never) what etiquette books call a 'lady'. It is very difficult. One thing keeping me from achieving my goal is that I am totally unwilling to give up the pleasure of eating icecream on the street. This is deeply frowned upon or at least strongly discouraged in anyone hoping to pass as a proper lady. To me, it is one of life's greatest pleasures.

I adore icecream and water-ices and never miss a chance, no matter what the season, to treat myself to one or the other – after lunching in a restaurant, for dessert when I have guests over for a meal, or for a snack at a café. But the greatest pleasure of all is a big scoop of soft, creamy icecream swirled into a peak or filling a crisp cone which enables you to set to right away, without having to wait for a spoon (which anyway is an unnecessary implement that only gets in the way).

There is nothing better than walking down the street on a sunny afternoon in June with some icecream. The city is in holiday mood as the first warmth of summer envelops you, and draws young people out on to the street and into the icecream shops. The feeling that a new season is upon you fills the air and with that feeling is the longing for summer to arrive in earnest. You can almost taste it in the soft, fresh flavour of lemon and strawberry icecream, and in the delicate colours of walnut and pistachio. In fact, you can almost taste its essence as you bite into the last bit of the cone, where the icecream never quite reaches.

Some cones have cleverly avoided this problem, compensating somewhat for the usually inferior quality of their icecream and for the fact that the cone and its contents were not put together a moment ago right before your eyes. These manufactured cones are made for the teeth, not the palate, and they are filled with ice-cream right down to the end. They make you want to suck out the icecream through the tip, something which is not very easy and certainly not very elegant. And it goes completely against the rules for behaving like a lady. Yet sometimes it is impossible to resist.

To stroll along with an icecream in a cone or on a stick is one of life's little pleasures. It is one that can be enjoyed in all innocence and with no regard to age. It is a pleasure that can be shared alike with a friend, a lover or a child. But, best of all, I think, is the pleasure of eating icecream alone. Then you can concentrate better, find your own rhythm, set your own pace and complete the methodical destruction of that pleasure, so ephemeral and so brief. If a rose lasts but for a morning, how much more transient is the pleasure of an icecream?

Each time I eat an icecream, it brings back other ice-cream memories from my past. For example, there was the one that I ate, with great pomp and circumstance, with my mother, in the most elegant icecream parlour in my home town, sitting very straight in front of a multi-layered bowl served on a shiny tray. Or the one I had years later, one evening after dinner with friends, in a famous old icecream parlour; we ate our icecreams leaning against a railing and looking out at the lights in the harbour. I remember too my wedding cake, which in honour of my sweet tooth, was made of icecream, apricot and cream, by the best home-made-icecream makers in town. Then there was one, never-to-be-forgotten *trompe-l'oeil*, which was made to look like a pink watermelon with flecks of bitter chocolate trans-formed into seeds. My memory then picks out an unforgettable, intoxicating, jasmine icecream that I discovered once on a trip to the south of Italy and never found again, though this had as much to do with the fear of being disappointed as anything else (some things are best left as memories). Lastly, and most recently, comes a spectacular one, a sizzling golden crêpe that arrived with a trickle of vanilla icecream melting on the plate.

Yes, indeed, there is no end to the surprises in the world of icecream. And that is part of its beauty. Industry and craft have never stopped inventing, creating and fashioning new dishes. But perhaps we, the *aficionados* – and I am first among them – should admit that the most traditional tastes and most classic pairings are still the best, although this should not keep us from getting involved each time with the full kaleidoscope of possibilities. It is a game with a thousand choices. Like sculpture, icecream should reveal all its facets and forms to our imagination: icecream cakes and flans; icecream tubs and moulded icecream; lollies and parfaits; hollowed-out shells of fruit filled with water-ices; velvety fillings in sponge cake; meringue playing with vanilla and chocolate icecream; profiteroles and fritters . . . and who knows how many other special creations.

The kingdom of icecream has many loyal subjects and even a select band to sing its praises. Folco Portinari, the author of this book, is certainly a great devotee and he took no time at all before agreeing to become one of the poets in that select band. 'I will be glad to talk about icecream,' he said. 'I will not keep my memories secret. I will give them full rein. I'll probably end up saying a lot of personal things, too many even. But that's the only way I can do it, because the subject is too tied up with my childhood and with my relationship with my family, especially my father.'

How could it be any other way? When talking about icecream one cannot be a detached reporter, a dispassionate chronicler of the news, because the pleasure of it, the emotional involvement, the memories it conjures up are too strong and compelling.

I, too, without even wanting to, have begun Folco's avowedly personal history of icecream with a personal declaration of my own.

It's funny. People often say that icecream is a child's food. I don't believe it. I have seen children, napkins and bibs around their necks, stuffing themselves with cones, bowls, bars, and lollies a thousand times. Think of the mess they make. They are terrible consumers of icecream. They cannot even finish their serving. They get tired before the end. They get everything dirty and end up even stickier than usual. And, worst of all, they let the icecream melt in the bowl until suddenly they grab their spoons and start madly stirring together all the different flavours, making an undefined sludge of flavours and colours, completely ruining the consistency.

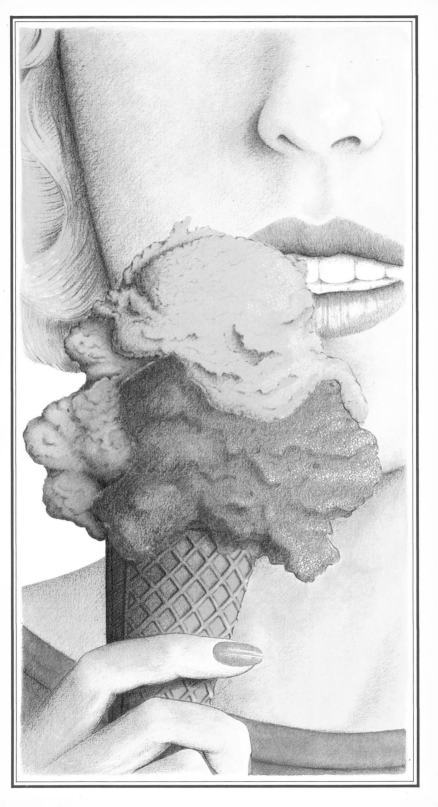

No, children are not true icecream lovers because they lack an essential ingredient: memory. The true icecream lover is a mature person who chooses her or his favourite flavours with seriousness and determination. They eat it with just the right rhythm to keep the creamy consistency of the icecream or the tart liquid of the water-ice. They keep it not too soft and not too hard – for too much hardness would hurt the teeth and above all impair the ability to savour the full flavour and aroma.

In summer, icecream is often the pretext for an outing, an excuse to have a bit of fresh air, or to meet a friend. In many countries, icecream parlours, with their little tables and chairs, are one of the classic attractions of a very traditional pastime. They have long been social meeting places and, in their respectability, they remain somewhere where one can go to see and be seen. Unfortunately, it is also true that there are those outdoor stands where cars can pull up, stinking of petrol and oil and making terrible noises; this does not add much to the delicate smell of raspberry or vanilla icecream.

Sometimes, then, it is better to go home and enjoy

some icecream in your own garden or in a big armchair in the living room. These days there are machines that can make icecream in a jiffy, but if you are really lazy or just very impatient, all you have to do is open the freezer door and, with any luck, you will find some there. I always keep on hand a triumphant icecream flan or an elegant icecream sundae in a tall, clear glass just in case friends drop by, and I like to serve refined sorbets in a big silver bowl, so I can savour those 'moments of concentration' with a 'discreet clatter of plates, a cautious and silent movement of spoons, like a solemn ceremony'.

So, *viva* icecream, old and new, the icecreams of yesterday, today and forever, the icecream that feeds our small grand passion.

MARIAROSA SCHIAFFINO

CHAPTER I

WHY DO WE LIKE ICECREAM?

Oh sweet sorbet,
Precious delicate nectar,
Bless the person who made it.

Carlo Goldoni,
Amore in caricatura,
a drama for music, Act II

The Need to Cool Off

FIELDS of snow or glaciers were for centuries the sole solution to a problem that was not only physiological (how to cool off in the heat), but was also related to the quality of goods (how to keep perishable items cold). An example of how far back this problem (and solution) existed was shown when a huge ice house was discovered in 1986, during some excavations in Italy near a university in Milan: it was the ice house of an ancient convent.

How and what happened? The procedure was quite simple: during the winter, snow was collected and packed into a pit that had been dug out in a spot which received little or no sun. Often this was in a cave or a stone pit. When the weather became hot again, there was a ready supply of ice to turn to.

It was an ancient technique and one practised in many countries, including Great Britain. An Italian at the end of the eighteenth century wrote: 'There is little more to say about the ice houses. We make them as the ancients did, digging deep into the earth and filling the hole with ice or snow that we pack down into it, after which we cover it with branches of oak and straw, like Athenas and Seneca did and Saint Augustine after them in "The City of God". . . Laonde Simonide says. . . that the snow is buried alive for in that way it can be preserved and thus make the summers bearable and, when buried, it becomes a thing of grace and beauty.'

So there were genuine ice repositories in those days

and they survived for years in the countryside, even after machines were invented to keep things cold. And not so long ago in the cities huge blocks of ice were still being dragged on horse-drawn carts, and delivered to households to be put into an ice box, and all sorts of methods used to keep it from melting. And then, refrigerators came along. But that was not until much more recently.

Sub-zero Science

Ice even more than snow, allowed people to satisfy and eventually to popularize the otherwise impossible thrill of feeling something cold on the palate, the enjoyable illusion of coolness, a moment's deception in the hot sun – pleasures which, until now, were available only to the wealthier classes.

We can certainly thank the bedouins for this, for in the middle of a blazing desert, they will put water in a pan, cover it with a wet cloth and leave it out in the sun

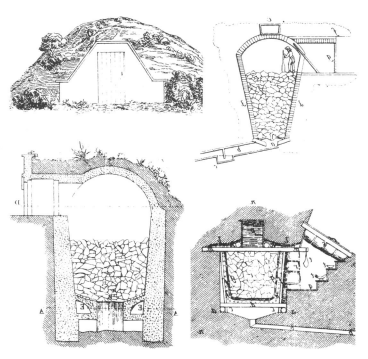

Designs for nineteenth-century ice houses

to cool. Yes, to cool. 'Experiment No 1': the anomalous idea that you can cool water by exposing it to the Saharan sun (the bedouins also wear wool clothing!). This suggests the law that regulates this occurrence: the evaporation of water from a damp cloth steals heat from what it covers. This in fact is similar to the principle governing the workings of refrigerators. I must admit it seems like magic to me, going against all reason.

We should also thank Robert Boyle who in 1632 presented to the Royal Society in London a study of refrigeration. And above all we should thank Michael Faraday who in 1823 established a definitive history of the changes in the physical state of gases, which allowed J Peckins in 1834, J Harrison in 1856, and in 1875 the German, Linde, and the Frenchman, Pictet, to construct their refrigeration machines. Thanks to these we can today enjoy pleasures that would otherwise be impossible.

Here I would like to interrupt with a personal recollection.

I would like to tell you about an invention that must be really ancient if someone as old as I am can remember it from his childhood. I remember how my father or my brother would sometimes come back from the city (we lived in a very small village at the time) with icecream from a famous icecream parlour wrapped up in a package and surrounded with a strange substance that stung you when you touched it: it was dry ice. 'Solidified carbon dioxide', said my brother the chemist, 'CO_2'. In 1892, there was already a factory in Italy, in Pergine. Even today, I still do not understand how it works. But I do know that it can help keep icecream solid for a certain length of time, a few hours at least, which is enough time to get it home and enjoy it (it can also be used to great effect in films and the theatre to make smoke and clouds). A wonderful invention with many uses.

Remembrance of Things Past

There is no doubt that we are talking about a pleasure that helps avoid or limit the effect of pain or annoyance or disagreeableness. You feel cold? Put on a fur coat. In this sense, eating icecream is a 'negative' pleasure, since

'The Art of Making Icecream', a delightful eighteenth-century
French etching

you do it in reaction to something negative (excessive heat). But there are also 'positive' pleasures to it, for it is one of the regressive pleasures that take us back to our childhood. Icecream is an indirect way of recapturing time past and the sweetness of those primordial sensations. We each have our own rituals and memories that we use to conjure up the past but for me the most subtle pleasure, the most authentic and sublime pleasure of all is icecream.

For Matthew, my grandson, icecream is normal everyday food, nothing special, no different from anything else (is it possible, I ask myself?). It is part of his school lunch. Not so for me. My father did not allow his children to eat icecream for reasons of hygiene, so I developed wild cravings for the substance.

I also have a scarcely dimmed memory of the icecream man who pedalled his icecream wagon from place to place, a white wagon with gaudy coloured stripes, whose front end was shaped like a swan, like the figurehead of a boat. To announce his presence, the icecream man would ring a little brass bell similar to the ones used today to signal a train. Icecream in two sizes came out of a machine, one which fascinated us children, because it could press out icecream sandwiched between two thin wafers. There was also the mythic cone with its bizarre scroll-like appearance, full of ripples to help out the tongue. Two different licking techniques depending on which one you chose, cone or sandwich, were required. After all, icecream is about licking, with the tongue serving as a go-between, helping out in the important jobs of slurping and sucking.

Icecream was affordable in those days which demonstrates how much icecream had already expanded its market, even before it reached the point where it is now available to everyone. But, a hundred years ago, it was expensive, if not a luxury. I recently came across a note that I made during a speech: 'Many years ago, a cup of coffee was threepence, a cold drink fivepence and a water-ice eight.' Four times more than it was in my day, but also almost three times as much as a coffee.

But nostalgia is not enough to explain icecream's widespread popularity, even if it does play a role among us old folks. So let's turn back to the present.

The Senses at Play

Why do we enjoy a childish pleasure whose qualities consist of sweetness? And when you add cold to sweetness, it becomes even more complex. And this is still not enough. Today we can give our pleasure flavour, all sorts of flavours, fruit flavours reproduced from the first garden of delights. And then there is milk. All this allows us to choose and mix things which naturally and culturally delight us and make them into something cool – water-ices and icecream. And then we lick them and continue the makebelieve, by assuming a typically infantile pose, reproducing the impression of a baby suckling at its mother's breast, with all its temptations.

Taken this way, the most genuine icecream, the one with the most symbolic meaning, is the one in a cone. And, in fact, it is also the most universal symbol of icecream. It is not by chance, either, since the cone permits a subtle almost intimate contact with its creamy substance through the use of that perfect organ, the flexible, soft and supple tongue, the tongue with all its implied functions, metaphors and characteristics, sensual (as the seat of the maximum concentration of gustatory senses) as well as sexual.

As if that were not enough, the tongue also lets us prolong the pleasure, thereby giving the most enjoyment, by its varied and enthusiastic licking techniques. Icecream is a delicacy made for licking, like a child sucking its fingers. However, the image of licking is not altogether innocent or neutral, especially when practised by grownups; it carries certain metaphors and allusions. The images produced by little Matthew licking an icecream and by Brigitte Bardot doing the same in the 'fifties are quite different.

Is a cone then a symbol of the nipple? Or is it some other trick of our memory? Actually the patiently licked cone seems to me to be in state of decline today. It has been modified by a number of factors that have transformed icecream radically from its main purpose, which was to relieve us from the heat of summer.

Icecream used to be seasonal and water-ices even more so, since they depended on seasonal fruits. And this is the point. By their structure and their very purpose, icecream and water-ices were part of an ancient seasonal tradition which technology, with all its systems of preservation and transportation, has managed to abolish. They have become something we can eat at any time, food that is analyzed in terms of calories and composition. Forget icecream's historical value and its connection with ice and thus its diverse physiological and psychological history.

That icecream eating has evolved in this way should not surprise us too much (it would be surprising if it were different), since it is part of a large, complicated evolutionary process which belongs with the 'industrial society'. It would be foolish to deny this evolution or even oppose it, with hopes of an impossible return to the past. That is clear enough. What we must not do is to feel regret. Instead we should try to understand what is happening.

Icecream in January, Moscow-style
So what do we have in compensation? The appeal of summer, of holidays by the sea? All is not dead and gone

'The Icecream Eaters', a nineteenth-century lithograph by the
French painter, Louis Boilly (1761–1845)

after we have buried our memories. What we think of as hot and cold is relative anyway. To appreciate this, you need only take a trip to Moscow in January. A normal everyday occurrence (and for us a rather civilized one) is the long patient lines of people waiting in the icecream bars and food stores to buy icecream cones, usually vanilla. Outside the temperature is $-22°F$ ($-30°C$). So icecream, at $16°F$ ($-8°C$) is warm by comparison.

Does this mean that this 'simple pleasure' has been absorbed and assimilated into a great machine and served up as one more ingredient in the great existential-industrial-economic megastructure? Not a chance, because the simple pleasures in life are personal and can only be enjoyed with fantasy, in the imaginations of each one of us, independent of anything else. So, don't worry!

Snow-covered Moscow

CHAPTER II
A HISTORY OF FREEZING

NOT being a proper historian, I will not attempt to write a complete history of ices. I will simply try to give you some highlights. At the same time, however, I want to remain faithful to my original idea of writing about the pleasure of the stuff, the small cold pleasure of icecream. This forces me to go back to my own childhood to my initiation into the mysteries of icecream, which I think is analogous to the infancy of our civilization. Let me explain. In my village during the 'snows of yesteryear' (it really did snow: it is not just a trick of my memory), we used to delight in an age-old custom of filling up a glass or cup with snow and pouring some red or green syrup or lemon juice on it, making a very rudimentary but natural water-ice.

A Cup of Snow

I like to think that water-ices or sorbets were born in a brimming cup of snow, perhaps mixed with some fruit or a little honey, and stored in a snowdrift. Sorbets could have gone on like that for centuries, in a process of constant improvement, which is something even I have done my little bit to advance.

It was said of the typical ancient Greek that 'the more cold beverages he drank, the stronger and more vigorous he became, wherefore he remarked that he filled his glass with snow from Mount Olympus'. So, there you have my childhood cup of snow. Also in ancient Greece 'sometimes snow or ice was served that was crushed and put into a glass to cool a liquid that was in it. Then there was Tyne, king of Paflagon, who every time he supped, wanted a hundred animals of every kind ... and in similar numbers, other smaller ones, and with them enormous blocks of ice so that for his entrails burning from the overflowing amounts of food, he could keep iced drinks chilled' and 'Cleopatra, in a banquet prepared for Mark Anthony, wanting to show her magnificence spent a great sum of money on pure snow'.

Is it Latin or Arabic, Sorbitium or Sharbet?

In spite of all this, however, sorbet does not have a clear date or place of birth. There is not even an absolutely certain etymology. Even its citizenship is precarious, though some, perhaps for reasons of misplaced nationalism, want to connect it to the Latin *sorbitium*. What was *sorbitium*? It was something to sip, like a broth, but it was, more specifically, a food, if you could call it that, in a liquid or semi-liquid state. On the other hand, sorbet, through tradition or custom, is also attributed to the Arabic, from the word *sharbet* which comes from *sharab* meaning 'to drink'. So, whether *sorbitium* or *sharbet*, its form was more or less the same, with the most common definition being a cold drink of fruit or honey (or a kind of Roman mead), and this form lasted a long time. If we go along with the idea of sorbet being Arab in origin, (within the context of the complete historical darkness which surrounds and circumscribes it), its diffusion in Europe would inevitably begin with the Moorish domination of Sicily and Spain. This seems the most likely beginning of the sorbet in Europe. I do not mind repeating this story, though the documentation about it is rather scanty and is as uncertain as it is for other types of icecream.

Some Twelfth-century Recipes

A twelfth-century Arab book called *Andalucian and Almohad Cookery* was recently found in Seville, and it has some interesting recipes for different kinds of sorbet. One type of sorbet it calls a *juvaris* and this appears to be based on concentrated fruit juice that is chilled after cooking, and the sugar allows the juice to become candied and thus, preserved. Here is a recipe for a *juvaris* sorbet flavoured with red sandalwood: 'Take three quarters of an ounce of red sandalwood [*tabasir*] and one quarter of an ounce of sugar. Mix it with one pound and one quarter of an ounce of sugar [*sukkar*] mixed with rosewater. Cool it until it has the consistency of a *juvaris* sorbet and remove it.'

Another recipe for *sarab* mentions 'sorbets of pomegranate, green grapes, citron, dates, blackberries and other fruits', which had been prepared in Andalucia since the eleventh century. The *sarab* is prepared in a similar way to the *juvaris*: the fruit is cleaned, filtered, cooked, skimmed, mixed with honey or sugar, cooked again and left to rest for a week.

A sorbet of fresh roses is made as follows: 'Gather a pound of fresh roses and. . .cover them with boiling water for a day and a night until the water cools and the petals come loose in the water; strain them and be sure they are clean, then add a pound of sugar and cook it all together to get the consistency of a sorbet.'

Finally there is *al-sarab al-farah al-kabir* that might be translated as the 'sorbet of great happiness'. The recipe: 'Take some borage, some mint, some citron leaves, about ½ ounce each. Cook them all in boiling water until they release their "force". Then filter this and add to it a pound of sugar. Then put in "the bag" a piece of aloe, a bayleaf from Sind, cinnamon from China, cinnamon and cloves, a spoonful of each. Soak it all, put it in a cloth, close it tightly and put it in a pot, letting it macerate until it releases its "force"; then cook it until it has the consistency of a sorbet.'

As you can see, it is not a matter of running off immediately to try out the recipes (though perhaps as an experiment, I might just try it, with all the respect due to our elders), but of appreciating this very old gastronomic document as something that can capture our attention in spite of the centuries that separate us.

The Renaissance

We continue in darkness with semantic doubts about the word 'sorbet' (that is, in finding a meaning similar to ours today), until the Renaissance, with not negligible gaps along the way. Its history, though with visible uncertainty, can and should begin here. This is when, for example, a greater and better understanding of the use of sugar began, which was fundamental in the making of sorbets and icecreams. But even here we must be cautious, because much is repeated from hearsay, one document quoting another, when documents were very rare. In truth, there has been a lot of nonsense written about the subject and much repetition of error carried from one unreliable source to another. At the top of the

list of historical confusion I would place the Medici affairs, attributing either to Catherine de'Medici or to Maria de'Medici the taking of icecream from Florence to the French courts, after everyone has agreed to award the architect Bernardo Buontalenti the prize for this invention. As written, at the end of the eighteenth century: 'Bernardo Buontalenti, a man of great understanding and very well known for his genius and for his many marvellous discoveries, was the first to make ice boxes. But the use of iced drinks was not immediately accepted. They were disdained by most as harmful to one's health and condemned by doctors as difficult to digest and disturbing to the natural heat of the gastric juices in the stomach. But then human ingenuity, made wise and clever in matters of eating, discovered that this beverage instead of being harmful was actually very healthy.'

Sugar and Salt

It is equally important to learn about the machines that freeze liquids by using snow mixed with salt. This was based on the discovery, according to the laws of physics, that salt lowers the temperature of the liquid.

I happened to come across a recipe for making a sorbet in a text from the second half of the seventeenth century.

It says: 'To make twenty jars of lemon sorbet, you need three pounds of sugar, three and a half pounds of salt, thirty pounds of snow, three lemons if they are large and if they are small, you will have to be the judge, particularly in the summer months.'

Another discovery of mine (and this perhaps is the reason we attribute ices to Buontalenti) suggests how water-ices first evolved into icecream: through the use of sugar and egg whites (which are used as a binder by painters in tempera) plus milk, all beaten together.

What is certain and must be taken into consideration is that the icecream machine stayed the same for centuries. It consisted of a central cylinder into which were put the ingredients; the cylinder was surrounded by another container filled with snow or ice and salt; and a paddle or something similar was then used to turn the substance continuously until it froze. All machines were based on this design.

An Italian Product and a French Glory

If ices were born in Italy, their invasion of the world began when they went to France. And here finally we have a central episode in the so-far nebulous history of

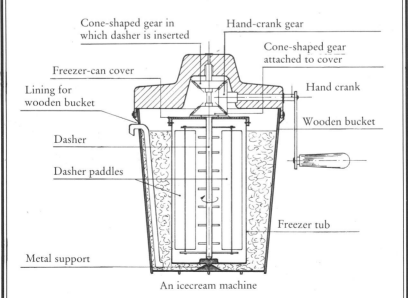

An icecream machine

sorbets, with precise dates, real people and even a geographical location. This was the arrival in Paris in 1660 of the Sicilian, Francesco Procopio de Coltelli, who opened a café, the Procope, that would prosper for three hundred years after he died. Who was the real Procopio? An article written in July 1970 says 'his family seems to have descended from the German Umfred di Messer, who came to Sicily as a major-domo to Frederick II [in the thirteenth century]. In Sicily the surname "Messer" which in German means "knife", was translated into Italian as Coltelli or Cutelli, which is the Italian word for "knife"'. Be that as it may, and we will give the writer the benefit of the doubt, there did exist in Paris in rue Fosse in St Germain, now rue de l'Ancienne Comédie, a Sicilian named Procopio who had an open-air stall in the second half of the seventeenth century which would become a famous café in the following century, serving the likes of Prévost, Marivaux, Rousseau and Voltaire.

This, then, seems like a solid reference point even with all the vagueness surrounding it. Another thing that was certain was that the French court of Louis XIV, the Sun King, was a model for every other court in Europe. And a final point, at the dinner tables of the Sun King's court, people enjoyed water-ices and icecreams (whether or not they had been handed down by the Medicis or had come through the sorbet maker Coltelli). And from there, icecream spread outside its confines to the rest of the world. A text by Louis XIV's 'pharmacist', Sieur Lemery, was translated into English in 1685 and in one of its chapters ('Sweets, Flowers and Fruits') it gives recipes for sorbets.

In *The London Gazette* in 1688, one can read an account of a party given in Stockholm by the English ambassador Edmond Poley on the occasion of the birth of the Prince of Wales: 'After the meat was taken away, a very refined dessert was served with great pyramids of sweets in which were contained all varieties of fruits and icecream that the season permitted.' In England, icecream was brought from France with the return of the exiled Charles II (an anecdote relates that a life annuity was given to Charles I's French cook after he served him an icecream).

Not only kings but books crossed the Channel; soon followed cooks since something very much like a school

Refining sugar in a sixteenth-century print. The syrup obtained
from the can was put into conical moulds

of gastronomy was evolving in France. In fact, a whole
culture was developing. In *La maison réglée* (1692)
Adiger explains how to use moulds to form fruit
pyramids; Massialot in 1698 explains 'how to freeze all
kinds of water and liquors' and in 1718 discusses what
shapes to give to icecreams and sorbets to disguise their
identity. La Chapelle, who also wrote about the subject,
studied and extended the discourse on decoration as well
as concerning himself with the quality of icecream. 'Even
if the task of making sweets is not specifically mine,' he
wrote, 'I possess some knowledge and experience in the
art . . .'

A Luxury for the Rich

So, it is apparent that ices were becoming a solid citizen
in some parts of Europe. But it must not be forgotten
that they were still a pleasure limited to the tables of the
aristocracy and the bourgeoisie because of the difficulty
in getting the basic materials, snow and ice, and the
consequent high cost of production. In fact, most
cookery books were written by cooks employed in the
houses of nobles. The aforementioned La Chapelle, for
example, was in the service of Lord Chesterfield before
changing to the Prince of Orange. Charles Carter, the

author of the *Complete Practical Cook* (1730) had been the cook of the Duke of Argyll, the Count of Pontefract and Lord Cornwallis. And so on. The modest circulation of icecream can also be documented by the fact that the word did not enter the French *Dictionnaire de l'Académie* until 1762, and then always as a plural, *glaces*. However, in Diderot and d'Alembert's *Encyclopédie* (1751–72) there is a full description of the word *glace*: 'modern name given to a pleasant-tasting liquid ably prepared and frozen to a soft slush. All the liquids obtained from vegetable juices can be quickly frozen, by using chipped ice and salt, or in the absence of salt, with saltpetre and soda'.

What then was the most common way of making ices? 'They take milk pots especially made for this in large numbers; these are filled to the brim with liquid specially prepared from seasonal fruit. . .They put a number of these pots in a bucket with or without compartments about a finger's width apart: around it they put crushed salted ice until they are completely covered.'

Of course, if a quicker cooling was desired, they would use a larger quantity of ice, taking care that the salt did not get into the liquid in the pots. 'After stirring all the pots and their liquid in these containers, they are again covered with their lids and then with more ice and salt, as before. The more salt put on the ice, the faster the liquid freezes; the pots are removed from the bucket only when the icecream is ready to be served.' At the end there is a last reminder: 'I am aware that in Italy, that beautiful country where the preparing of it is an art, most doctors, rather than condemning it, assure us that its consumption is very healthy.'

As confirmation that icecream was gradually becoming more widely available, we can add a quotation from the third edition of the *Encyclopaedia Britannica*, that of 1797, which, describing a method for making ice-cream, says: 'Take enough cream and if you want to mix it with raspberries or pineapple, take a measure of juice or marmalade equal to a quarter of the cream, beat it and then filter it through a cloth, and add to the mould some drops of lemon juice. The mould is a pewter glass of different sizes and shapes. Cover it and put it in a bucket that contains two thirds ice to which you have

A Venetian sorbet maker in the eighteenth century in a drawing by
Pier Leone Ghezzi

added two handfuls of salt. Rotate the mould, holding it by the handle with a rapid movement back and forth the same way you would beat chocolate, for eight or ten minutes. Let it rest for half an hour and it will be ready to remove from the mould and serve at the table. Lemon juice and sugar and juices from various other fruit can be frozen without using cream. If you are using cream, you must mix it very well.'

Such admirable precision!

The Arrival of Technology

The spread of the two varieties, sorbet and icecream, water and milk, formed a clear pattern. It was a split between fruits and flavourings. The two families branched out. It was natural, of course, that fruit and thus sorbets, took hold where fruit grew in abundance – places like the Mediterranean, the Ottoman empire (Turkey to Arabia), Spain and Italy, while icecream was the choice in the northern countries and in the English colonies. Thus icecream came to America.

Some claim that the first to bring it to America was an Italian, Filippo Lenzi, who set up shop in New York in 1777 where he sold icecream. But there are documents which mention a Barbara Jannsen, sister-in-law of Lord Baltimore and wife of Brandon, the governor of Maryland, and say that she served it with great success at a reception in 1744. A guest described it: 'We had a dessert no less curious; among the rarities of which it was compos'd was some fine icecream which, with the strawberries and milk, eat most deliciously.'

It is true that this was probably an exceptional case because the adoption and diffusion of the sweet came later, when it was often served at gatherings with the French during the American Revolution (Lenzi resurfaces at around this time too). The Americans preferred icecream to sorbet, probably because of their English heritage. A dinner served by the wife of Malexander Hamilton included 'pyramids of red and white ice cream with punch and liquors, rose, cinnamon and parfait d'amour'. In fact, Americans are so fond of icecream that today it has become virtually a national food, as anyone who has ventured to those shores will know.

It is difficult, if not impossible, in such a small space to give an exhaustive history. What is important, however, is to observe how, beginning in the nineteenth century, the history of icecream coincides with the evolution of technology rather than with matters of taste. And American technology played a not negligible role in this development.

But let us jump back again to 1751 when Hannah Glasse, the author of one of England's most famous cookery books, *The Art of Cookery Made Plain and Easy*, gives us a point of reference on 'how to make ice cream'. She writes, 'Take two pewter containers, one larger than the other. The smaller should have a tight-fitting lid in which to put your cream that you can mix with raspberries or whatever you wish. Then close the lid tightly and put it in the larger container. Fill the larger with ice and a handful of salt; leave it so for three quarters of an hour; open it and stir the cream well; close it again and leave it in the ice for another half hour, after which you can serve it'.

Is there anything new here? Yes, there is a pewter container (instead of wood), the absence of eggs, and a second mixing forty-five minutes after the first. This system continued to be used until 1846 when Nancy Johnson invented a freezer with a crank which is still used by many families. The patent for this very important machine, the first mechanical icecream maker, was taken out in 1848 by William G Young. The secret lay in the possibility of stirring the mixture for a sustained period, allowing it to freeze uniformly and preventing the formation of ice crystals.

The Spread of Icecream

What was happening? The methods and recipes split and multiplied, that is true, but the real story now lies in the spread of this delicacy, in the popularization of a product that had hitherto been enjoyed mainly by the élite. For this is now what happened, and it was made possible by mass production. The true artists remained in Italy, while marketing strategies (and eventually the technology) developed elsewhere. There is the oft-told story of Jacob Fussel from Baltimore, to whom the birth of commercial icecream is attributed. Fortuitously, Fussel, a milkman, having a huge surplus of milk, transformed it into icecream and his success was so sensational that he decided to open an icecream store. It was the first brick laid in a new industry. For this alone he deserves a monument.

The experimental period in the history of icecream making, the age of 'exploration', ends here. In the next century, a new stage begins, the use of technology and management to resolve the problems of production and distribution. Thus we reach the industrial age and the great advances in machinery.

The first important industrial system to be invented was refrigeration, and the manufacture of ice and

Florentine sorbet sellers in a nineteenth-century French lithograph

refrigerators, which we have already mentioned. During this period, the new crafts were developed to a very high level, becoming a culture of their own. This technology behaved like a centrifugal motor of enormous proportions and it led to icecream becoming a typically Italian phenomenon, just like spaghetti and pizza. From Cadore, from Friuli and from Sicily, Italian icecream spread throughout the world, and with it went icecream-making machines.

The Expansion of the Product

At this point, another story begins, no less interesting if not quite as important as that of the pioneers. This is the story of the growth of new varieties of icecream, which, as it developed, created innovations and encouraged the use of the imagination in developing more new products as well as new techniques and technologies. Often, like an ancient song, information about it was handed down orally, with all the attendant risks of such a system.

The chronicles of the time report that at the Universal Exhibition of Paris in 1900, visitors were attracted by giant machines that made ice and produced cubes of flavoured syrup. It was a clever idea for publicity and a good idea for a product.

A 1950s' advertisement for the first mass-produced icecream in Italy

[33]

There is also a controversial anecdote. At the beginning of the century, an Italian, Vittorio Marchionni, emigrated to the United States and, along with his brother, bought a factory in New York and one in New Jersey. Here they invented nothing less than the icecream cone (which to me has always borne a magical resemblance to the hats worn by fairies and magicians, even if it is upside down). Their claim to have invented this has been challenged by the Americans who preferred to credit it to Charles Menches or to a Syrian, Ernest A Hamwi. The time and place: 1904 at the St Louis World Fair. For once the interest in the container rather than the contents was not misplaced. For this rolled wafer, in the shape of a cornucopia, was a mythical symbol and it is said that in the 'twenties in the USA 500,000 cones were made a day.

By putting a serving of icecream between two wafers you get an alternative to the cone. This is the creamy icecream 'sandwich' I bought from the icecream wagon of my childhood. In Italy it was called a 'Parisian' and

A nineteenth-century Italian sorbet seller

its invention was attributed to one Giovanni Torre who emigrated from Liguria to Paris. I notice that after an eclipse of a few years, the 'Parisian' has again become popular, no longer using the thin wafer of my day, but with a more solid biscuit.

And what about the ice lolly or the bar of icecream on a stick? Another American, Harry Burt, seems to have been the creator, yet I remember it as a novelty just after the last war, around 1951, when Motta, a big Italian icecream manufacturer, seized on the idea and produced their own version which they aptly called a *mottarello*.

In Milan they didn't start manufacturing icecream on a large scale at all until after the Second World War, but within thirty-five years the yearly *per capita* consumption of that town leapt from 9 ounces (250g) to 13 pounds (6kg).

An example of icecream's unstoppable progress.

CHAPTER III
THE WORLD OF ICECREAM VARIETIES

IF YOU consider all its varieties, icecream has almost as many possibilities as bread, perhaps even more.

It can be moulded into all sorts of different shapes, disguised, dressed up, subjected to a range of aesthetic (and not so aesthetic) treatments, tinted any colour of the rainbow, and even made to challenge the very laws of nature itself by being served hot. It can also be sculpted into thousands of different shapes. This variety is due in part to the fact that the laws of the marketplace demand a constant flow of new and innovative products. But the endless possibilities for manipulation also reached a peak during the golden age of icecream and sorbets, when they were luxury foods that appeared only on the tables of the rich. In those days icecream was moulded into architectural shapes, sculpted, decorated, and played with as much as the material would allow. Its consistency was the same then as it is today so it was imagination which made the difference. There were *trompe-l'oeil* creations to fool the eye by imitating fruit and flowers. A classic example of the first was an orange which was cut open, hollowed out, filled with orange-flavoured sorbet and then closed again. It is a whimsy that has survived until today and has been used with other fruits such as the lemon, the melon and even the coconut.

These were but little tricks and small surprises. In Adiger's *Maison Réglée* of 1692, the technique of vitrification is described. This consisted of filling a pair of tin moulds with icecream, which would then be unmoulded to form a pyramid, the top to be garnished with icecream frozen into fruit and flower shapes. The pyramid was formed with the careful selection and arrangement of different-coloured icecream.

We can divide frozen desserts into three basic groups: sorbets (made with syrups or fruit juices and water), fruit-flavoured sherbets (which may or may not contain milk) and rich icecreams (which are made with milk or cream, eggs, sugar and flavourings). Each kind has its own subdivisions, such as granitas and slushes, milk shakes and sundaes, flans and *bombes* and parfaits. (Basic recipes are to be found in Chapter VII.)

The Suave Sorbet

As the first born, we must put sorbet at the top of our list. The sorbet has always had a rather ambiguous nature, name included. Sometimes it is considered a beverage and sometimes it is considered a solid food. Articles have been written extolling both its virtues and its dangers to digestion when taken as a cool interlude during a heavy meal. But then people thought of hot drinks in the same way. Today, however, when we no longer sit down to dinners of gargantuan proportions, it seems to me that sorbet has resumed its proper place, even when it is served drowned in spirits and liqueurs such as vodka, grappa or kirsh. The humbler granita is a slushy, semi-solid drink and, in its coffee flavour, it is often served in summer in the south of Italy as a kind of late-morning breakfast, topped with cream and accompanied by biscuits.

Sherbets and Icecream

The thicker consistency and the combination and variety of ingredients of a sherbet sometimes makes it difficult to distinguish it from fruit icecream. It maintains a delicate balance between solid and semi-liquid, with a consistency that borders on the creamy. With rich icecream, however, there is no doubt. It has a definite, velvety creaminess which puts it in the category of food, not drink. Thus it can be integrated into a meal with other more traditional food, even substituting for some, and should be accepted as a dish in its own right.

Recipes, formulas, methods and traditions used in making icecreams, along with all the variations and contrasts that go with them, suggest endless fantasies. And I think they are all legitimate. The most common modification is the addition of a little liqueur to a plain-flavoured icecream like vanilla. To give icecream your personal stamp, simply add a little grand marnier, chartreuse, rum or any other fruit- or nut-flavoured liqueur, or 'drown' it with a little coffee.

I remember how, long ago, I used to finish off my dinner parties with vanilla icecream topped with gratings of white truffles.

From Dish to Cone

Leaving creative and nostalgic diversions aside for the moment, let me say that for me the right place for ice-cream is in a dish, preferably with two scoops, combining either complementary flavours (chocolate and nut) or contrasting ones (chocolate and lemon, for example). What then happens inside the dish, especially if it is a shallow bowl perched atop a long stem, is simply indescribable. For the ultimate experience of this kind, we should go to America and see what happens in that country. There we can behold a multi-coloured mass of icecream covered with hot fudge or butterscotch sauce or strawberries, then topped with what looks like a cloud over Mt Olympus made of whipped cream, and as if that were not enough, punctuated with a maraschino cherry or a sprinkling of chocolate bits or chopped nuts. This is America's national dish, the sundae. A delicious monument to opulence.

Still, the best way to enjoy icecream as food is the way they do it in Sicily. There they eat it as a sandwich between two pieces of sweetened bread or in a brioche, perhaps adding a thin layer of marmalade. Yet, if it did not sound like sentimental pretence, I would confess that my heart still lies with icecream in a cone – one that I can lick (and eat, if the wafer is good), and icecream in a cardboard tub, surrogate for the lovely crystal dish.

Nor is this from snobbery, but from pleasure. Even the huge icecream industry has realized the potential of this collective memory, an association that the younger generation would affirm as well: icecream and cones go together. Today's ready made cones are compact, and some come covered with a coating of chocolate or a sprinkling of nuts; others might be stuffed with cherries and syrup.

I have already mentioned several of the many varieties of icecream in a dish and how they reflect the whims of their creator. A few have reached international status and can be found on menus around the world – at which point their origins have usually been forgotten. I think of the belle Hélène in which vanilla icecream is married to a poached pear and both are covered with chocolate and garnished with Chantilly cream. Or of another famous creation, the Melba, where a peach cooked in syrup rests on a base of vanilla icecream. It was named after the Australian singer Helen Mitchell Melba, who was called Nellie. The great Auguste Escoffier invented this classic in July 1899 at the Carlton Hotel in London. The peach for this dish must be of the white variety, ripe and fragrant. It is poached for two seconds in boiling water and then plunged immediately into icy water. Aftewards, it is peeled and placed in a dish over vanilla icecream and covered with a purée of raspberries. There is some dispute about the raspberries and Escoffier himself writes in his *Unedited Memoirs*: 'Some take the liberty of substituting strawberries or currant jelly for the raspberry purée. This does not give it the right flavour at all. Even worse is the lack of seriousness

of those who thicken the raspberry purée with a floury paste. Others would decorate the peach with whipped cream . . .' No, Miss Melba would tolerate only raspberries. Anything else is a fraud.

Moulded Icecreams

We can go on and on, but the list would never be complete and we would add nothing new to the basic concept. It is better to turn to something else, to another type of dessert, one which has perhaps stood the test of time. The first name that comes to mind is the parfait. Its very name means perfection, achieved through a harmony of ingredients and a delicate creamy flavour. The same is true of *bombes glacées* and mousses. The three are similar and all use a mousse-like base of egg yolks, sugar, cream and whipped egg whites. The parfait and the *bombe* (which actually does mean 'bomb') betray their antiquity by reminding us of the days when bombs were shaped like balls. The *bombe*, made from spherical moulds and filled with various flavours in concentric layers, was in fact inspired by the anarchists. Here is a basic recipe that can be used for either a parfait or a *bombe*.

You will need 12oz (350g) sugar, 10oz (280g) water, 16 egg yolks, 1lb 11oz (750g) whipped cream, and flavouring or liqueur. Mix the sugar and water, bring the mixture to the boil and boil it until the sugar dissolves, then let it cool. Add the egg yolks and cook the mixture in a bain-marie for about half an hour. Then whisk it until it is cool and add the flavouring or liqueur and the whipped cream. (The *tartufo* is a ready made version of this recipe, though smaller and covered with chocolate.)

Let us now return to the south of Italy, the cradle of icecream, and look at some famous and celebrated concoctions. There are three in particular from among the many unforgettable ones, that I find interesting.

One is the *spongato* which is sorbet enclosed in a rum-soaked sponge cake. A close relative is the *pezzo duro*. This is a kind of frozen pudding made by packing ice-cream into a broad, flattened cylinder, and then cutting it into individual portions. Similar moulds in France were called *fromages*.

Acireal is known as the birthplace of *spumone*, two flavours of icecream, one inside the other. That on the outside is either chocolate, vanilla or pistachio flavoured and the one on the inside is made from egg yolks whisked with sugar until golden yellow and foamy (hence the name *spumone* which comes from the Italian word *spuma* meaning 'foam'). *Spumone* is moulded in containers shaped like half a hemisphere, as is the cassata.

'Cassata! Oh, what delight, the heart wavers/One bite is enough/Just the very name makes me jump with joy/ And when I taste it, I reel with Hope . . .' Here, we will wave the Sicilian flag a moment as we explain the ice-cream version of the cassata, that illustrious dessert which in its original form is made with ricotta cheese mixed with candied fruit and chocolate. The icecream version consists of three alternating layers of vanilla, pistachio and Chantilly icecream covered with sponge cake. Both versions are round in shape and go back a long way. Their name comes from the Arabic word *quasat*, or 'round bowl'.

Desserts and Cakes

The cassata is part of a group of desserts made with ice-cream, which brings us to icecream cakes. But here we enter the wide, uncharted waters of personal creation. However, I prefer to steer clear of these and to head back to the more defined shoals of traditional recipes, even turning to very old ones. A hundred years is not such a long time ago, but in a relatively brief history such as this one, it is. If I look back a hundred years I come to *Scienza in cucina* by Pellegrino Artusi, an extraordinary testimony to middle-class Italian cookery.

Artusi gives a lot of space to the subject of icecream and three of his recipes in particular catch the eye. The first is for a 'biscuit' or 'frozen ball' that starts with a base (made with egg, sugar and water) which, 'beaten till thick, has cream slowly added to it', and ends up 'frozen . . . between a layer of ice and salt'.

The second one is *ponce alla romana* (Roman punch), which was an icecream 'of recent invention that is served at important luncheons before the roast to help digestion and to predispose the stomach to receive the rest of the meal without nausea'. Water, sugar, oranges, lemons, egg whites, rum and vanilla are the ingredients, but to prepare it you must go to recipe 770 in that sacred text.

There are many other desserts I could mention. A Neapolitan might fairly complain of the absence up to this point of the *coviglia*, a semi-frozen, foamy substance eaten from a metal cup (egg yolks are beaten with sugar and flavoured with whatever you like, and then mixed first with whipped cream and then with beaten egg whites). Honoré de Balzac might protest that I have neglected the *plombières*, which are similar to *tortoni*, in that cream is cooked with chopped almonds, milk, vanilla, and lemon peel over a low flame and then strained. The flavoured milk is then mixed with egg yolks beaten with sugar, to which can be added candied fruit and bits of chocolate once it condenses. From Genoa, my wife's home town, comes the offended cry, 'And what about *paciugo*?' This is a concoction of vanilla icecream flavoured with black cherry syrup. From America come the supporters of the icecream sundae, the icecream soda and the banana split. And I can hear the British crying 'What about brown bread icecream?', a curious but delicious British invention. As for the rest of the world, well, all we are lacking is a Norwegian who demands that I include his omelette . . . (see Chapter VII).

Fire and Ice

The Norwegian omelette reminds me of another subject, hot icecream desserts, which reach an extreme in mysteriousness and intellectual compromise, rhetorical figures of daring execution combining two apparently irreconcilable opposites, hot and cold.

The one I know best is not baked Alaska but the *taglio*. This is a bowl of vanilla icecream with hot coffee or chocolate poured over it, the close relative of another icecream dish in which icecream or lemon sorbet is drowned in a spirit such as grappa, vodka or whisky – a beatific means to inebriation.

Inventions, inventions . . . And on the subject of bold inventions used to great effect, I will close this brief and incomplete selection with the flambé. This is the extreme in terms of fire and ice, unless we literally throw ice cubes on to the fire. The best way to explain what it is, is to give you the recipe just as I received it from Angelo Paracucchi, a master cook. The ingredients are 9 very ripe figs, 2 oz/60g sugar, 1 glass kirsch, juice from half an orange. Put a pan over a flame, add the sugar and let it foam. Add half the kirsch and light it, then add the

figs and orange juice. Shaking the pan, add the rest of the kirsch, letting the alcohol burn off. Fill bowls with a soft icecream and add a few of the flaming figs. Let the rest caramelize and put it on to the bowls. Raspberries, blueberries, strawberries, oranges or pears can also be used to good effect. At this point, you are limited only by your imagination.

Tradition and Novelty

There is one area of the icecream world where products are rarely very original in concept – in fact they are all quite similar – yet in terms of production it is an extremely important area. I am talking about commercial icecream. In a modified way, icecream companies offer many of the same products that we have enjoyed traditionally. At the same time, the industry has confronted and resolved its special problems of mass distribution and preservation so that today we can buy all kinds of ready made products at the supermarket, even local specialities. There are versions of soft icecream and there are icecream cakes of all kinds and shapes. Today there is something for every taste.

CHAPTER IV

A THOUSAND TEMPTING FLAVOURS

. . . to reward them there was an icecream cake.
It was raspberry but it was more than raspberry:
Combining its freshness and moisture
With its scent,
It melted in your mouth,
Disappearing as when the snow melts
In the meadows, and
Everything becomes spring water.

Charles-Louis Philippe
Croquignole

FLAVOUR is crucial. Given the huge selection available (of colour as well, a functional coefficient that is part of the pleasure), we can choose a flavour to satisfy a sensual or a psychological whim – indulging our taste buds or our curiosity or a sense of adventure. This is its beauty. 'What flavour do you want?' 'I'll have vanilla and walnut . . . no, make it vanilla, chocolate and chocolate chip.' A familiar dialogue to the person scooping up the icecream at a shop selling icecream. But has it always been like that? We know it has not, or rather we know that in recent years there has been a visible evolution.

Those of us who can, remember that the unforgettable icecream wagon of the past had only a very limited selection of flavours. One was the prototype of the sorbet. The list I have in my memory for icecream tells me pale yellow meant creamy vanilla, brown was chocolate, white was lemon, pale pink was strawberry and green was pistachio.

In the best-stocked icecream parlours one could also find a nut-flavoured icecream and a nougat one, while sorbets, by reason of their ingredients, were always fruit flavoured, and predominantly lemon; cassatas and *zucottas* were restricted to vanilla and nut. This completed the entire range.

Icecream, Icecream Everywhere

What is happening now? The most diverse, unthinkable flavours are being invented. Fruit flavours in particular have gained favour, thanks to the advance of health concerns (by now almost every town or city has a shop that boasts of selling icecream made only of pure, natural ingredients, uncontaminated by chemicals). This is easy to understand, since fruit obviously suggests 'nature'. The implicit psychological thrust is to link it with thoughts of the country, natural products, simple flavours, the subconscious idyll.

Of course, you are not thinking of such things as you lick your icecream cone, but that does not mean they are not there. Is there any flavour that has not been tried? I do not know. I do know that today along with old-fashioned strawberry and old-fashioned lemon are offered watermelon, peach, apple, pear, apricot, plum, black cherry, cherry, blackcurrant, raspberry, blackberry, blueberry (and what about 'fruits of the forest'?), pineapple, banana, papaya, kiwi fruit, melon, mint, walnut, hazelnut, almond, pistachio, orange and mandarin orange. The list is probably incomplete and we could add to it those extravagant icecream fantasies made – for better or for worse – with yogurt or liqueurs.

One no longer marvels at anything: there is an extravagant Italian inventor in Turin who accepts no limitations. He experiments, successfully it seems, with icecream flavours that go beyond the realms of the imagination, and include celery, wine and gorgonzola, a witness to the unstoppable drive of the omnivore.

Rich icecreams come in as many flavours as there are things that can be added to the basic recipe: chocolate, chocolate chips, chocolate with toasted, chopped nuts, *marron glacé* with bits of candied chestnut, bits of nougat, bits of chopped hazelnuts, bits of After Eights, and rum and raisins. Faced with such a variety, there is the risk of falling into the same predicament as the legendary ass who could not make up his mind what to eat and ended up starving to death. Once more one looks to the past for salvation, going back to plain chocolate and vanilla, or vanilla and lemon, or hazelnut and chocolate. Or being even more radical and simply choosing only chocolate or vanilla.

The cacao plant in an eighteenth-century print

The situation with sorbets is not very different. If the number of choices has not been quite as large as with icecream, it is only because sorbet itself is less widely available in Britain and the United States. It is more common today in homes and icecream parlours in Mediterranean countries, where the traditional flavours are lemon, coffee and mulberry. From the earliest lemon-flavoured ones, the range has extended to include other citrus fruits, especially the more delicate mandarin orange, but it also includes the kiwi fruit, green apple, pear, melon, strawberry and fruits of the forest, all delicate flavours. These flavours go well with spirits that can be frozen such as vodka, pear William and framboise. One can even put these liqueurs directly on the sorbets, as a friend of mine does every year at his parties, making a sorbet with grappa.

But sorbet is not just limited to fruit. A good example of its flexibility was given by a friend of mine who has invented – and this is the only word for it – a meal in which every course is accompanied by a special sorbet, such as tomato, spinach, carrot and so on.

Showy exhibitionism with its colourful and elaborate creations is part of the history and enjoyment of icecream. This is true not only in Europe (where the Germanic countries tend towards baroque tastes), but also in the United States. I think in particular of those lavish colourful concoctions served in long-stemmed dishes, full of icecream and fruit and covered with sculpted mountains of whipped cream and sprinkled with syrup and chopped nuts. A sense of plenty, of richness, of abundance, of the peak of satisfaction and fullness is implicit in that bowl. Of the original icecream there would seem to remain only the word. Its very creation transforms it into an object of contemplation, intended more for the enjoyment of the eye than of the palate.

Friend or Foe?

When we choose a combination of flavours, we seem to follow certain elementary but unspoken rules – perhaps out of habit. On the one hand, there is an element of daring, curiosity and adventure, a desire to try new things. On the other hand, there is healthy scepticism, a refusal to join the crowd, and a reliance on memories and repetition. Between these two extremes, flavours are combined either because they are similar or because they make good contrasts. So you might put fruit with fruit, mixing fruits of the same sort together, or combining cream with cream, water with water or milk with milk. There is no need to study this very deeply. My grandson Matthew already knows these rules instinctively. Those who like contrasting flavours put milk and water together, exemplified in the marriage of chocolate and lemon mentioned at the start of this chapter. Advice? Do whatever you please. How much we would miss if we were not free to enjoy things as we please, especially such pleasures as food.

My Favourite Icecream Parlours

I have pursued and will continue to pursue the pleasures of the palate even with all the travelling and moving I have done. When I was young, I did my apprenticeship in Italy's Turin. In those days the king of the city's icecream parlours was called Pepino (it still exists today);

[49]

it lay in the piazza Carignano in front of one of the most extraordinary baroque monuments anywhere. This place was the best of its kind, and I still like to visit it, in that quiet little piazza, when I return to my home town. A very worthwhile and pleasing homage.

At the opposite extreme, lies the youthful chaos of a provocative and inventive icecream parlour in via Cernaia, the one that has experimented with gorgonzola icecream (but not wine icecream). More controversial still is the Sicilian place on via San Quintino that has vegetable icecreams. In these places, you must be very careful about which flavours you choose to mix together.

I lived for a few years in Florence and there it was said that the English royal family used to frequent Vivoli's. But I loved to get in line for a cone at Gailli on the Ponte Vecchio.

Now I live in Milan. If I feel like something with fruit I go to Viel in the piazza Castello (the one that makes the most classic milkshakes). I also like Pozzi with its pleasant terrace in piazza General Cantore.

In other Italian cities faithful friends have introduced me to icecream parlours with long traditions. In Rome, I would not miss the Giolitti, near the Montecitorio, which has had an élite clientele since the days of the Marquise of Grillo. The truffle icecream is supposed to have been born here. Another place that draws many customers even though it is less central is Annunziata Fassi, with a garden and mostly classic flavours. For unusual specialities in an original atmostphere, you should visit the Selarum Societa Cooperativa in Trastevere, one of the first icecream makers to make icecream from exotic fruits and nuts.

Of course, all these names are given with a word of caution. Fame can corrupt anyone.

England

England is not Italy. Here, most commercial icecream is unlikely to stir the passions of the ardent icecream lover. But good icecream does exist. And there are a few icecream parlours here and there that serve it. In London, there is the Gran Gelato in Montpelier Place, Bernigra in Tottenham Court Road and Marine Ices in

Haverstock Hill. In the summer, Prestat, the chocolate shop off Piccadilly, also stocks marine ices or if you are in that neighborhood and you prefer to sit down to enjoy your icecream, Fortnum & Mason serves milkshakes, sodas and frappés. While you are in the shop, you should also look at their selection of packaged icecream. They carry two brands, Prospero, which makes lovely sorbets with flavours like champagne, and Donna's, which comes in seductive flavours like cointreau, drambuie, pink champagne and, for the old-fashioned, brown bread icecream.

The best way to enjoy icecream in England is to buy it in a packet to serve at home. And the biggest selection of top-quality icecream is – predictably – to be found at Harrod's, if you are willing to fight your way through the crowds. Besides the more widely distributed Loseley products, which are excellent, there is Harrod's own brand which has several liqueur flavours and a version of brown bread icecream, another brand called 'New England' icecream claiming to be a 'full cream recipe from Vermont', several French brands including one which offers lemons and oranges filled with sorbet, and even an icecream for diabetics made with fructose. There is a selection of icecream *bombes* and flans and some spectacular icecream cakes that you can have made to order for a special occasion (there is a charming ladybird

for example which would be delightful for a children's party).

If you are wondering what happened to such old-fashioned flavours as chocolate and vanilla, you can relax. They have all gone to Marks and Spencer which seems to carry little else but several kinds of chocolate and vanilla-flavoured icecream. They also have something they call 'American-style' icecream in outrageous flavours like 'Double Chocolate Chip Ripple'.

With the introduction of milk quotas, many farms have turned to making icecream and some of the results are excellent. It is worth looking out for these in local shops and restaurants.

Let us hope that a demand for high-quality icecream grows in England to such an extent that it will eventually be available in everyone's corner shop.

CHAPTER V

THE MAKING OF A MARVEL

ONE thing is clear: things have changed with astonishing rapidity in our industrial age. Technology has made it possible to sell icecream far and wide so that now its consumption is no longer an exception but an everyday occurrence. Has this happened everywhere to the same extent? No, the spread has been uneven. In Britain, for example, *per capita* consumption is only about a fifth of what it is in the United States. Italy is the same as Britain, which is even more surprising considering that Italy developed much of the technology and techniques for icecream making, and virtually invented the product.

But overall, the development of icecream's extraordinary variety has been matched only by the speed with which it has developed.

This development is no miracle. There are obvious reasons. The most striking is technological innovations. The homogenizer was invented in 1899, the circulating brine freezer in 1902, the continuous freezing process in 1913, and home storage freezers came out in 1940. From

Quantities of Icecream consumed per Country

USA
Australia
USSR
Canada
Sweden
Norway
Ireland
Denmark
West Germany
Holland
Belgium
Switzerland
Great Britain
Italy
France

there, storage systems developed that allowed a large-scale industry to grow and distribute its products.

This has transformed a product that was originally a highly perishable luxury to one that is within reach of the average consumer. And it brings with it all the dietary and behavioural consequences that we see today. Between the two extremes, industrial products and home-made icecream, there is still a middle ground, small icecream makers who do not mass produce their icecream, yet make a sufficient quantity by hand or with simple machinery to supply local restaurants and ice-cream shops.

Innovations and the Icecream Industry

The icecream industry has grown enormously, especially in the United States where over 900 million gallons (4,000 million litres) were produced in 1987. This is a statistic worth considering. Technological innovations have played a major role in the development of such large volumes of this product. But it also means that to maintain and expand this level of production, a complex strategy has had to be developed to maintain quality and the right price.

Industrial production in fact initiates a whole series of market-related problems. Above all, companies have to maintain close and constant ties with their consumers whether interpreting their demands or suggesting new products to them. Icecream is no different from any other industry. Manufacturers must constantly come up with new ideas and new products (new shapes, new combinations of flavour, new ways of consumption) without losing the interest or disappointing the expectations of the public. These products do not just depend on 'image'. They also have to perpetuate, even exploit, childhood memories, using icecream as a psychological point of reference, and at the same time balancing the appeal with innovative new products. There is a paradox here because the industry is not as open to experiment or constant change in its basic product as others might be. This is because manufactured icecream depends on preservation. And herein lies the paradox. Where, for example, gorgonzola icecream or celery sorbet are risks that a small icecream maker can afford to take from time to time, big commercial icecream makers must work on a much larger scale, where the risks are much greater. Yet the laws of marketing and even their own research and development departments demand that these manufacturers come up with new types and varieties to capture the market.

Development in the USA really started with a Mr Fussell, but when he started to make commercial icecream in Baltimore back in 1851, little did he know that it was the start of what would be a billion dollar business a century later. Setting the pace he opened up factories in Washington DC, Boston and New York. Others followed and hand manufacturing was replaced by mass production as new technology became available. Companies began to patent special products like the eskimo pie in 1921, the good humour bar in 1923 and the popsicle in 1926. Tom Carvel invented a soft icecream that he sold from vans; this was widely imitated and even today the music from the icecream van can make a child run for her or his pocket money.

Today, in America, after decades when commercial icecream grew cheaper as artificial ingredients were substituted for natural ones, full-cream icecreams have returned with as much fanfare as they can muster. Haagen-Dazs started it by offering higher-priced, better-quality icecream through franchise shops all over the country. Smaller local icecream shops, like Ben & Jerry's or Steve's Ice Cream, known locally for their high-quality product made on the premises, grew famous as rich icecreams became the fashion. And the icecream wars of the 1980s were on as each vied with the other for a bigger share of the market. The battle still rages, but surely the ultimate victor will be the consumer, whose supply of high-quality icecream is assured for years to come.

A Visit to an Icecream Factory

The factory I visited is in Parma, Italy, and it is called Italgel. I should add that it could have been any one of a number of factories, because I believe that they all run in much the same way. The important thing was not which factory I saw, but actually to see one in person, to experience it directly, even though there was a risk that, like a child, I would come away more with the wonder of it than with much pure knowledge.

I started my visit by reading all the ingredients on the packet, which listed all the raw materials. Then I visited the warehouses where the raw materials, in industrial quantities, are kept. My eyes were struck by the yellowness of the butter and the deep orange of the frozen egg yolks. There was milk, cream, powdered milk and vegetable oils. And I saw the fresh fruit that the fruit flavours are made from. What beautiful colours they produced, especially in the soft icecream – I felt attracted to them just as a bee or a butterfly is attracted to the bright colours of a flower. Somehow, their colours seemed more intense than usual. The person who was leading me through the factory was honest. They used colour intensifiers he said, but these were made from natural colourants such as beet extract or chlorophyll or carotene – even the additives there are made from natural ingredients.

At this point the wondering child turned back into an adult and realized something which prejudice often denies: big business does not always want to risk its image by using less than the best ingredients. It is not worth it to them. Another concern, no less important, is that which rendered icecream making so difficult when I was young (and which so worried my father that he imposed strong restrictions on its consumption, ultimately provoking my own strange love affair with icecream). This is the problem of maintaining scrupulous cleanliness.

Icecream undergoes so many treatments from the start of its manufacture to the finish that it becomes immune from any bacterial risk: salmonella will find neither the space nor the conditions to grow. As the icecream passes from process to process, it is almost as if it is in an isolation ward. Those who work with it wear clinical gowns and little white caps to cover their hair. Hygiene appears to be the most important and prevalent consideration of all. I can rest easy now after seeing the attention given to this problem.

Did you Know that Icecream Matures?

The odyssey that the raw materials undergo has functional stages. These begin with mixing the ingredients at 120 atmospheres of pressure until they are homogenized, then they go to pasteurization. Then they must pass through a process of maturation. Yes, icecream matures. And here, wayfaring wine connoisseur that I am, in my meandering through the factory, I received a big surprise. Good heavens, here were the same stainless steel vats used to ferment the wines of many of my friends. There were seventy-four of these stainless steel vats, all in different sizes.

On-the-spot Tastings: the Pleasure of Quantity

Here the little boy took over, unable to restrain himself any longer, and was given an on-the-spot sample. All right, all right, keep quiet, you devils of cholesterol and calories, I will eat less for lunch. After all, icecream is food too. The sense of wonder continued, seeing the pineapple cut into little bits and stirred into a pineapple-flavoured icecream, with the addition of air, necessary to make it creamy. It was also wonderful to see all the other different flavours and combinations of flavours. And to watch the temperature drop from above freezing to way below freezing in minutes. And then there was an amazing cooling tunnel at $-48°F$ ($-45°C$) through which the icecream passed so that it would develop a kind of light crusting before being stored at $-14°F$ ($-27°C$).

Finally, there was the wonder of sheer quantity. It is not that I do not know that an industry is what it is because of its high level of production. I know this but it does not affect the disorienting wonder I felt looking at twenty-two beautifully packaged products that were turned out in just a few minutes. It is true that the technicians were amazed at my amazement, but the difference between us was that I was playing at being an explorer. I stopped to look at a vanilla-flavoured block of icecream that was gradually transformed, first by being encrusted with a layer of peanuts and then covered with chocolate. And there were icecream flans and truffles, and crêpes full of vanilla icecream, all exquisite in

themselves, but also delicious as desserts with enriching homemade additions.

But the child, the protagonist of this industrial adventure, could not help but be struck dumb by wonder when confronted with the old-fashioned shapes, the ones from his childhood. Part of this wonder came from discovering that they were still made. The cones were my own form of 'madeleine', and there they were being plroduced at the rate of 20,000 per hour. There were also ice lollies on sticks, 12,000 of them produced per hour.

And what's this? It is a new invention, a pseudo-cone in the shape of the Statue of Liberty's torch. Unbridled imagination on the assembly line.

Finally we must not overlook the computer that runs it all. This Wizard of Oz is a complicated command station with flashing red and green lights and a big computerized brain not unlike those that regulate the movement of trains in and out of Waterloo Station. Twenty-two products, twenty-two tracks. 'And on track five, the ice lollies for . . .' A child's paradise.

CHAPTER VI

IT'S GOOD FOR YOU
AS WELL AS GOOD

And no one will ever know
That in the pink and violet icecream
I have eaten the lovely adventuress
Cut into pieces, slowly, greedily,
With a small silver shovel
And that she had a flavour
Like frozen raspberries . . .

Corrado Govoni
'I Ate a Girl in an Icecream'

AT THIS point in my icy pleasures, one thing has become clear. Sorbets and icecreams are one of the oldest and most beloved of our small (or great) pleasures. *Homo cupiens.* Perhaps this is because sorbets and icecreams seem naturally to go hand in hand with oppressive weather. They compensate for such seasonal or meteorological sufferings as heat, sultry weather or thirst.

Obviously, the subject of modifying, foiling and relieving the heat with cool or frozen drinks has been debated and discussed for centuries. We have old documents about this filled with arguments based on science, custom and commonsense. Refrains from old disputes are quoted here and there in this little book, showing the close connection between gastronomy and medicine in the past, especially evident in the high value placed on the stomach and gastric systems as the source of health and well-being. From the stomach, our predecessors moved on straight to the soul, for, as they said, a sound mind leads to a healthy body.

Pleasure or Pain?

Our pleasures may be simple, but their effects rarely are. Many things have been written down the centuries on the virtues or otherwise of consuming icecream and cold drinks. I include just a few examples below.

[61]

I will begin with one from the second half of the thirteenth century: 'Cold water is very harmful when taken with fish bait because it chills the stomach and makes everything indigestible'. The allusion is to a fish swallowing water as it takes the bait, with tragic results for the fish. The message boils down to 'Don't drink cold drinks when you eat'.

Similar negative advice was given in 1586 by Doctor Castor Durante who, in his *Tesoro della sanita* (treasure of health), advises the elderly not to drink cold water because 'it is very harmful and it is impossible that he who drinks it often will not fall into old age and cold illnesses'. He also says that 'one must take care not to drink wine that has been cooled with snow or frozen water because it damages the brain, the nerves, the chest, the lungs, the stomach, the intestines, the spleen, the liver, the kidneys, the bladder and the teeth' (which covers just about everything).

However, a book which came out in 1775 says, optimistically: 'Through experience, we know that chocolate sorbet is a very good remedy for atrophisms and scurvy. Every so often, it is true, these maladies derive from acrid or bilious or chlorine salts. But chocolate sorbet is also very effective with gout-like pains that are indeterminant and fleeting. I have seen not infrequently that it has miraculously lifted the spirits of a hypochondriac or a melancholy person because of its youth-giving oils which are so good for the nerves.'

I do not know the scientific reasoning that lay behind these assertions, but I do know that a chocolate sorbet makes me happy and that melancholy and hypochondria just do not seem to go with an icecream cone. Again, in the eighteenth century, another writer pointed out that 'not at once was the use of iced beverages accepted . . . [For a while, it was] . . . detested by most people as harmful to their health and condemned by doctors as a disturbance to digestion and the stomach's natural temperature. But then human industry, made wise and ingenious in matters of gluttony discovered that iced beverages instead of damaging, refreshed the health, etc'.

More recently we read that: 'Icecream is less dangerous than a glass of iced water because it is swallowed slowly and thus does not bring about rapid changes of the blood in the mucous membranes of the stomach. After a sumptuous meal, tonics and stimulants for digestion often appear. One should never abuse them. Those made of cream and chocolate are the least digestible and fruit should not be to acidic. Weak or convalescent people should have melted fruit icecream in a big glass of bitterish wine.' With this unusual suggestion, we have even increased our collection of recipes.

Elsewhere I have talked about prejudices, mostly relating to health and hygiene, and I have also digressed somewhat to tell you of certain ideas my hygiene-conscious father held about sorbets and icecreams to which I was both witness and victim. He tenaciously adhered to the theory that what protected one from the cold also protected one from the heat and thus he believed that it was more thirst-quenching on a hot day to drink a cup of tea than to have an icy granita. This theory might possibly make sense in physiological terms but not in relation to pleasure and the imagination. With all due respect to my father and to Louis Pasteur I protest saying, 'But that's mad! A cold slushy drink! My kingdom for a cold slushy drink!'

Three Kinds of Icecream

Many things have changed over time, both from a technological point of view (to reassure those concerned about microbes) and from a dietary one. It is now time to mention the legal angle, since the European Economic Community has proposed (without yet making it a law) a classificaion of icecream by composition. Icecream will be divided into three categories:

1 Icecream (5 per cent milk or vegetable fats, 55 per cent milk, 30 per cent dry residues).
2 Milk icecream (2.5 per cent milk fats, 55 per cent milk, 25 per cent dry residues).
3 Cream icecream (7 per cent milk fats, 70 per cent milk, 32 per cent dry residues).

The real novelty of these last years when you compare them to my childhood has been a new attitude on the part of the consumer. This is the result of several things.

Industrialization has provoked a new attitude towards icecream. The constantly changing and developing science of food has stimulated change in the market for icecream. The result is that in the collective imagination icecream is no longer the luxury it once was but is now considered to be a food. Where it once was the exception now it is the norm. This is not a bad thing. In fact, it is a good one (and this is not just because of the supposed virtues of sorbet as a digestive interlude during meals). It is practically a revolution, with predictable economic and sociological effects. In restaurants it is the dessert I hear ordered most often, regardless of season. This means that the world has changed its sense of the nature of icecream. It is no longer seasonal nor exceptional.

Nutrients and Energy: Icecream is Food

Let us use a hypothetical sample of 4oz (100g) of vanilla icecream. This contains 10 per cent fats (eggs, milk, chocolate, nuts) 22 per cent sugar in the form of sucrose and glucose, 4.4 per cent protein (milk, eggs), 35 per cent lactose, 0.8 per cent minerals, and 0.3 per cent additives. From the lipids you will obtain 90 calories, from glucose 103 calories, and from the protein 18 calories. So for 4oz (100g) of icecream, you will get approximately 211 calories, which is about the same as 1½ eggs, 11oz (300g) of milk, 7oz (200g) of lean beef, or 2oz (60g) of pasta.

Air is always added to give the icecream a smooth consistency, pumped in during the freezing stage in commercial icecream or produced naturally when it is beaten. In both cases, the amount varies from 50 per cent to 30 per cent (a discussion of the effect of too much air, as when one measure of liquid becomes two and a half measures of icecream – and there has been much written about this lately – belongs to another book, one on sophistication and dietary cheats).

Of course, the proportions above vary according to the quantity of ingredients used, especially milk, cream, sugar and eggs. In a sorbet in fact the drop in fats, protein and calories (165 for 4oz/100g) can be sharp, but it is compensated for by an increase in vitamins. Certainly after a rich meal, a sorbet is better than a rich icecream, for obvious reasons.

This is what the revolution has been about: the discovery that icecream has widespread and varied uses, not only in terms of its hedonistic pleasure-giving qualities but also in its nutritive value, as an energy giver. It can be eaten as a snack between meals or as a dessert. It can be served as a course in a meal or even at breakfast, as another way of enticing your child to have her or his daily requirement of milk (especially for children who are not enthusiastic eaters) or it can be a way for you to eat your fruit, in the form of a sorbet. These are not such strange ideas. In the USA icecream is a part of daily life.

But as I finish this discussion I do not want it to sound, because of my enthusiasm, as if icecream were a kind of miracle cure-all, good for every occasion and use. No, all I want is to establish a very simple concept: icecream is a food like any other, with great energy-giving potential. Or at least it is rapidly becoming so. This does not mean that it does not have drawbacks and particular requirements like any other food. One must remember to eat it slowly, preferably along with other food and not alone, so that it does not stop the secretion of the digestive fluids (which can in fact be painful. This is a spasm that greed can sometimes produce). This just reinforces the value of licking it slowly, which our bodies always knew was the right way to eat it. For the same reasons of good sense, one should avoid eating too much of it. Naturally this is true if you have a negative reaction to it, but then you must rely on your doctor to tell you when you can eat it and under what conditions. In any case, it makes sense to look at the ingredients so you will know when it is safe to eat and when it is better to pass it up. (This last advice is mainly for those with weight problems, high blood pressure or diabetes.)

I cannot finish without one last recollection. I am reminded of the pleasant promise of reward we hold out to children for the pain and suffering they undergo when they have their tonsils out: 'Don't worry, it's all right, you have to eat lots of icecream afterwards.' When it happened to me, that 'afterwards' was enough to make me stoic and heroic in the face of surgery.

CHAPTER VII
MAY I OFFER YOU SOME ICECREAM?

IF TECHNOLOGY has shaped and increased industrial production of icecream, it has also made it much
easier to make icecream at home. Home-made frozen
confections have been in existence for a long time, but
in the past, they were limited by the complications
involved in making them. Today, however, the home-
appliance industry has made it possible for anyone to
prepare icecream for dinner, as easily as they prepare the
starter and main course.

Electric icecream makers are readily available and
come in all price ranges. (You can even buy an old-
fashioned hand-cranked one, a relic of another era.) So
everyone can make icecreams and sorbets at home
quickly and without too much effort. The beauty of
these machines, as sophisticated as they may seem, is that
their basic principle is substantially the same as the one
that Nancy Johnson discovered long ago; the original
icecream maker was simply refined and mechanized. It
still consists of mixing chilled ingredients together until
a frozen homogenized substance is produced.

Yet this has achieved a breakthrough. It means that
icecream can become part of the family's daily diet, and
is no longer thought of as a dish for very special occa-
sions as it was in the past. This creates a change of
attitudes, habits, and approach towards icecream and
sorbets that is almost revolutionary. It means certain raw
ingredients such as milk and fruit can be included in our
diets in an entirely new way. This possibility, I like to
think, will encourage the active creative side of the
usually passive consumer to explore new recipes and
experiment with the basic ingredients to come up with
new forms of this frozen food.

It would be difficult to give advice on which kind of
icecream maker to choose: the range, from the most
traditional sorbet maker to the most technologically
sophisticated machines, is wide.

A friend of mine would tell me to go to the devil for

An American advertisement of 1848 for the corn starch used in icecream making

using these modern machines because he will only make icecream in the old-fashioned way, refusing to be seduced by the comfort and ease of automation: 'Let it be established once and for all that icecream lovers should make icecream without using any mechanical means or artificial ingredients,' says he. 'You must create the right conditions so that you can make icecream exactly as it was made in Paris . . . by Procopio.' In that case, the only advice I dare give is: look at each machine individually, consider its virtues and drawbacks, and leave room for your own initiative.

The Hows and Whens

Is there an etiquette concerning icecream? At one time it was not considered proper to eat icecream in the streets, at least for adults. But one of the nice things

about icecream – whether it be in a cone or cup – lies precisely in the fact that you can eat it in the street today without creating a scandal or raised eyebrows.

At a luncheon, its place is as part of the dessert course. It is also suitable for a dinner or a midnight supper. It fits in perfectly with both a simple family meal and an elegant formal dinner. It can be part of a lunch eaten standing up at a counter or as a late-afternoon snack. There are really no limits.

There is one practice which I have seen lately, however, about which I must protest. This is the custom of serving a sorbet halfway through a normal lunch in a restaurant. It is a practice which comes from ignorance and a lack of culture. It is a relatively ancient custom which has been reintroduced along with certain other inappropriate gastronomical-historical revivals. In the old days, sorbets were served as a break in a pantagruelic feast, after about the fifteenth course. But that was quite different from what is being done today – serving sorbets in the pause between the fish and meat courses. This pause for sorbets came from a conviction that was held in the seventeenth and eighteenth century that something cold helped a full stomach digest its food: 'Sorbets, because of the sugar and the salt and cold must infinite good effects produce in our body, both in the digestion of food and in the impediment to blood clots.'

I have little more to add about serving icecream except to suggest that instead of using an ordinary small tea-spoon to eat it, you might consider trying one of those small shovel-like spoons. And, lastly, wafers and sweet biscuits are a refined accompaniment.

Nothing remains now but to roll up our sleeves and start our own experiments with icecream and sorbet. It is not possible nor would it make sense to try to give you every kind of recipe. The range of icecreams, the lists of ingredients and the methods for making them are all too vast. I will limit myself to just a few recipes, chosen either for their curiosity value or because they are good or practical. I will begin with one from 1733, for *fromage glacé* or 'iced cheese' (though it has nothing to do with cheese). It comes from La Chapelle.

Fromage Glacé

Bring to the boil a jug of about 2 pints of cream (just under 1 litre), sugar and a stick of cinnamon plus two beaten egg yolks; when it boils, add a piece of green lemon peel. Filter it and add a little orange-blossom water; taste it for flavour and sweetness; let it cool and put it all in a glass whose base and lid are surrounded by ice mixed with salt. Variations: add chopped pistachio nuts to this cream with the green lemon peel and then liquidize the cream. You can boil chocolate, coffee or tea with the cream.

Regarding sorbets, aside from the Arabic recipes, here is a quick recipe from a very old document, the *Carta Bardi II A.116*.

Citrus Sorbet

Bring sugar to a boil and leave it until such a time as when, adding a little water to it, it breaks like glass. And then begin to stir for the space of half an hour, adding to it as much juice as you want and as the odour pleases you.

Where it mentions 'juice', read lemon or orange juice.

For sorbets, the quantity of ingredients used varies according to the kind of fruit used. Take two extremes, the lemon and the pineapple. As we all know, the lemon is a very acidic fruit that contains little sugar. Thus the amount for lemon sorbet would be: 4oz (100g) juice, or 20 per cent; 5oz (150g) sugar, or 30 per cent; and 9oz (250g) water or 50 per cent. Pineapple on the other hand is a delicately flavoured fruit so the proportions would be: 4oz (100g) juice or 70 per cent (of which 10 per cent of the juice is sugar); 1½oz (35g) sugar or 23 per cent; a spoonful (10g) water or 7 per cent.

Thus the amount of sugar remains more or less constant while the amount of water used varies according to the fruit selected. Of course the amounts also change if, instead of the usual sucrose, you use some form of the less sweet glucose or an invert sugar which is sweeter and makes the icecream softer.

My next recipe is a homage to Sicily which I offer with thanks to Enrico Alliata, who gives many recipes for parfaits and icecreams in his vegetarian cookbook, *Cucina Vegetariana e Naturismo Crudo*.

Apricot Parfait

18fl oz, (½ litre) cream, 18oz (½kg) sugar, 18oz (½kg) fresh or canned apricots. Heat half the cream in a double saucepan, and when it is hot add the sugar, stirring until it dissolves. Take it off the heat and when it has cooled, add the rest of the cream, then freeze it. Peel and mash the apricots, then mix them in with the frozen cream. Stir it quickly for 5 minutes, then put it in a dish.

Nougat Icecream

2¼ pints (1.25 litres) milk, 11oz (300g) sugar, vanilla, 5oz (150g) amaretto biscuits, 6 egg yolks, 4oz (100g) cooked pumpkin

Put into a pan the sugar, egg yolk and a little vanilla, mixing them for 10 minutes. Then gradually add the milk and put the mixture over a low heat until it becomes thick and creamy. Mix in the pumpkin cut into tiny pieces and the crumbled biscuits, then let cool and freeze.

Personally I like nougat icecream best when I can bite into pieces of sticky nougat. I feel the same way about the little bits of candied chestnut in *marron glacé* icecream.

Now an embarrassment of riches weighs heavily upon me, because this is not nor can it be a list of basic recipes nor anything remotely resembling it. Rather I am relying on chance flashbacks of memory and in fact it is memory which suggests that I go back to a classic recipe by Vialardi from *Cucina borghese* (bourgeois cookery), published about a century ago. I found in it 'interesting advice concerning icecreams or sorbets' which says, 'if you find that your icecreams or sorbets do not solidify,

[71]

it is a sign that there is too much sugar in them and so you should add some hot water. Take care that if you want to add some spirit to the icecream you do it when the sorbet is frozen into a thick mass, because spirits will soften the icecream'.

For those who are faithful followers of tradition, I have copied for you from Vialardi this basic recipe for cream sorbet; it can be modified to suit your fancy.

Cream Sorbet

In a pan put 6 fresh egg yolks, 11oz (300g) white sugar, the thinly sliced peel from a ½ lemon or orange, 4 cloves and 1 cinnamon stick. Beat them all together with a wicker whisk until the mixture turns white. then add 1¾ pints (1 litre) of half milk, half double cream, and place it over the flame, stirring constantly. Do not let it boil. When it has thickened enough to coat a spoon, force it through a sieve, then let it cool, stirring it from time to time until smooth. Once cold, put it in a sorbetière. When it begins to freeze, add a stiffly beaten egg white, then let it finish freezing and serve.

I do not want to be accused of an over-zealous interest in archaeology. Some might say that today it is easier to go to a good local icecream factory or a supermarket and calmly choose from the variety offered there, thus resolving the problem simply and efficiently. Of course, this is true, but it is only partially true. In what shop would you find this marvellous coffee sorbet?

Coffee Sorbet

Pour 18oz (½ litre) unsweetened coffee into a pot and add 1 tablespoon cornflour, 9oz (250g) sugar, and 1 bar of plain chocolate, grated. Thin with a little orange-blossom water. Stir it all over a low flame until it is well blended. Then put it into a pan whose base has been lined with tender green lemon leaves and chill it till it thickens.

Perhaps you would like something more complicated, more sophisticated. Here, then, is a 'Maraschino-cherry-flavoured icecream *bombe* from the Terra Rossa made with Cabernet-Sauvignon-flavoured zabaglione', created by Gualtiero Marchesi, a delight worthy of a true master, and one that will earn you a reputation as a memorable host.

Maraschino-cherry-flavoured Icecream Bombe from the Terra Rossa
Ingredients for 2¼lb (1kg icecream)

1¾ pints (1 litre) fresh milk, 9 egg yolks, 9oz (250g) sugar, 5oz (150g) maraschino cherry syrup, 1oz (30g) icing sugar, 7fl oz (2dl) single cream, 12 individual dessert moulds holding 3½fl oz (1dl) each
For the zabaglione: 3 egg yolks, 3oz (80g) sugar, 7fl oz (1dl) Cabernet Sauvignon

To prepare the icecream: bring the milk to the boil. Put the egg yolks and sugar in a pan and beat them together with a whisk, then add the milk and blend it in quickly. Put the pot on the heat and let the mixture cook for three minutes, stirring constantly with a wooden spoon. Pour it through a fine sieve and let it cool. Then put it in an icecream maker and follow the directions for making icecream.

When it is ready, put the dessert moulds in the refrigerator for 15 minutes, then fill them with the ice-cream, making a well so that the sides and base are covered with a layer of icecream about an inch (2cm) thick. Put the cream in a bowl and whip it, adding in the icing sugar. Then delicately mix in the maraschino syrup with a spoon. Fill the moulds with the mara-schino-flavoured whipped cream and cover them. Chill them in the freezer for at least 3 hours (they will keep for up to 15 days).

To prepare the zabaglione: put the sugar and egg yolks in a pan, beat them with a whisk for 1 minute, then add the wine. Place the pan over a low heat (if gas, the flame should not come up the sides of the pot). Let the mixture cook for 2–3 minutes, beating the liquid constantly with a whisk. Then pour the zabaglione on to 12 small dessert plates. Remove the moulds from the freezer and briefly dip them into hot water, then turn them upside down over the zabaglione. Decorate each top with 3 maraschino cherries cut in half.

I also cannot help but be inspired by an extraordinary amateur cook, Livio Cerini di Castegnate, whose recipe for bilberry water-ice I hereby offer and recommend.

Bilberry Water-ice

This recipe can only be made in early autumn when bilberries are in season. I have never seen a recipe for it in any book or even any reference made to it. I think I must be one of the few who has ever made it. I should warn you that bilberries stain everything in a dreadful way – hands, shirts, trousers, towels – so some people might be understandably reluctant to work with them.

As soon as the bilberries are picked their stems and leaves fall off. Weigh the berries and then sieve them. Filter this purée 2 or 3 times. Dissolve 12oz (350g) sugar in 10oz (280g) water and mix this in to the bilberry purée to taste. For every 11oz (300g) bilberries used add also the juice of 1 lemon. Freeze the mixture.

This is a very special ice that you will rarely come across anywhere else.

It is hard, intellectually at least, not to want to maintain the pure culinary standards of the friend mentioned earlier. But to be honest, when I get hold of an electric icecream maker, I itch to use it. So then I turn to Angelo Paracucchi and choose an enviably light classic preparation that is absolutely delicious.

[74]

Basic Recipe for Rich Icecream

Ingredients: 1¾ pints (1 litre) milk, 18 egg yolks, 11oz (300g) sugar, peel from a ½ lemon (with pith removed)

Preparation: put the sugar and egg yolks in a pot and beat them together. Boil the milk with the lemon peel, then add to the egg yolks and sugar. Put the pot over a low heat and stir constantly without letting it come to the boil, until it thickens. Remove it and force it through a cone-shaped sieve. Then transfer it to your icecream maker and follow the manufacturer's directions.

This icecream is best if made the day before you intend to serve it so that the flavours have blended completely.

Using this recipe, we can begin to exercise our imagination and creativity. For example, if we boil the milk with coarsely ground coffee, we will have coffee icecream; with 4oz (100g) cocoa powder and 2oz (50g) sugar we can make chocolate icecream; by adding 7oz (200g) chopped almonds to the icecream when it is ready, we can make almond icecream (or we can add bits of nougat for a nougat icecream); for pistachio icecream, sprinkle 4oz (100g) crushed pistachios with milk, force them through a sieve and then add this to the milk and egg yolk mixture along with a little vanilla. And so it goes on.

As for fruit icecreams (not to be confused with sorbets), here is another basic recipe from Paracucchi.

Basic Recipe for Fruit Water-ice

Ingredients: 1¾ pints (1 litre) cold water, 1lb (450g) sugar, 14oz (400g) puréed fruit, 1 stiffly beaten egg white, juice of 1 lemon and its peel (with pith removed)

Preparation: combine all except the egg white in a bowl and stir to dissolve the sugar. Let it sit for a few hours. Then strain it through a cone-shaped sieve. Put it in an icecream maker and when it is thick, add the egg white.

If you keep in mind that the amount of sugar depends on the sweetness of the fruit, you can vary this recipe by using raspberries or pineapple, cherries or melon, or

whatever your fantasy dictates. As we saw above, excellent desserts can be invented with just a basic recipe – the sky's the limit.

The only thing left is that great contradiction, hot icecream. And that is just what we get in a way in the recipe below from Stefano Borghino for a 'Norwegian omelette'.

Norwegian Omelette

Ingredients: 11oz (300g) chocolate icecream, 14oz (400g) vanilla icecream, 11oz (300g) strawberry (or nut) icecream, 1 piece of sponge cake 9in (22cm) in diameter and 1¼in (3cm) thick, 3 egg whites, 2oz (50g) icing sugar, grated rind from a ½ lemon or orange
For the syrup: 7oz (200g) water, 4oz (100g) sugar, 4 tablespoons (50ml) orange liqueur

Preparation: cut the sponge cake into two pieces and round off the corners of one so that it forms an oval shape. Hollow out its centre, leaving a ½in (1cm) border around the edge. Fill this with the vanilla icecream, then make a second layer ½in (1cm) thick with the chocolate icecream and then cover it with the strawberry icecream. Crumble the rest of the sponge cake over the top, shaping it so as to look like a rugby ball. Put it in the freezer for at least ½ a day.

Boil the 7oz (200g) water with the 4oz (100g) sugar for 1 minute so that the sugar dissolves completely. Let it cool, then add the orange liqueur.

Heat the oven to gas mark 9/475°F (250°C) or use the grill.

Baste with the sugar syrup the top of the sponge cake that covers the icecream. Then beat the egg whites till stiff, add the icing sugar and the lemon rind and beat for another ½ minute. Using a rubber spatula, spread the egg whites over the sponge cake, forming a thin layer, then put any remaining whites in a pastry bag and decorate the top. Sprinkle the 'omelette' abundantly with icing sugar and put it in the oven for 2 minutes, till the top is golden.

Cut into slices and serve immediately.

A single flavour of icecream may be used instead of three different ones.

You may complain that I have left out recipes. I am well aware of that but I also know that once readers have tried these recipes they will be able to go off on their own and invent others. After all, these recipes only make sense if you try them out yourself. Good luck and I hope you enjoy them.

CHAPTER VIII

ICECREAM AND THE FAMOUS

A sallow waiter brings me beans and pork . . .
Outside there's fury in the firmament.
Ice-cream of course will follow; and I'm content.
Oh Babylon! O Carthage! O New York!

Siegfried Sassoon
'Storm on Fifth Avenue'

'ICECREAM? I could die for it . . .' This could have
been the epitaph of one of the master painters of the
eighteenth century, Jean-Honoré Fragonard. Fragonard
was representative both of his culture and of his era: the
court at Versailles from Louis XV to Louis XVI, the
mythical gardens of Eden and beautiful ladies in swings
that he painted, the golden age of coffee and chocolate.
Anecdote has it that he died of a throat ailment, from
love of icecream (although he was already seventy-five
at the time). He ate the fatal icecream, it seems, one day
when he was very hot. (May we learn from others'
mistakes!)

'Granita? I could die for it . . .' This could have been
the epitaph of the early nineteenth-century Italian lyric
poet Giacomo Leopardi, for he had a great sweet tooth
and he loved sorbets especially, or so said his friend
Antonio Ranieri. Ranieri wrote, 'His whole life was an
unrelenting series of vicissitudes to be endured; but the
anxieties and vicissitudes ceased when the doctors
forbade, with marvellous unanimity, most sweet things
and icecream completely. Longing for the one and the
other, he put aside any apprehensions and continued on
with the most incredible excesses . . . And as for icecream, there was wild enthusiasm . . . The more the
doctors threatened him with blood-stained sputum,
bronchitis and vomiting, the more his enthusiasm grew'.
This was the weakness of the flesh at work, unrestrained
by the soul and showing no regard for what Leopardi
called, in slightly ironic terms, *'magnifiche sorti e pro-*
gressive' (magnificent and ever-advancing fate). Here
was the materialist, demanding his due, and paying the

highest price for this last supper. 'After a few spoonsful of that rich broth, he stopped; and he asked the sister for an abundant lemon icecream that they call "granita" here. Paolina had them bring him a double. And, sipping it with the same avidity he had sipped similar beverages, after a moment he wanted to try the broth again. But it was too late.'

That icecream was 'good enough to die for' was almost demonstrated by another historical figure, the German chancellor Bismark who had a famous near-fatal attack of indigestion over a raspberry icecream.

However sorbets and icecream have not enjoyed the same good fortune among artists and poets that other delicacies have, perhaps for their perishable nature (they cannot pose immobile for very long). Or perhaps it is because they arrived on the scene fairly late, or because they did not become widespread until recently. While we can find mention of sorbets in thirteenth-century Mozarabic manuscripts, to find anything more about icecream, we must wait until the late Renaissance and then it is usually Continental – rarely British – travellers or authors of treatises who write about it. There are few literary or historical documents and, in the world of art, there is a total void.

For what we might call political reasons, icecream is spoken of in the accounts of Venetian ambassadors who maintained relations with the Turkish Middle East. For example, in the middle of the fifteenth century the ambassador Giacomo Soranzo described a meal with a sultan:

The meal was served one dish at a time, each on a large plate with bread, and each was a single food which, pleasing as it was, was taken and replaced by another; and so it continued, twenty-five courses between meat and fish, and with neither knives nor forks nor napkins on the table, and instead of a cloth on the table, there were rugs. The drink was a sorbet which is a composition they make of water and sugar with flavours and other ingredients not very pleasing to Italian tastes.

Not very different was this note by Garzoni from the

same period in *Piazza Universale*, a sort of half-serious encyclopaedia:

> We were led through a large doorway into the court-yard where we were to eat on the ground on a large rug where, reclining more than sitting, we ate something – so as not to show a lack of respect for their banquet – which consisted of bread, rice, beef and, unfortunately, a few chickens, and sorbets to drink in tin cups only once after the meal.

By now the sorbet was described more or less consistently as an iced fruit drink. One hundred years later, another Venetian ambassador, Sagredo, wrote:

> It is attributed to the greater economies of the Turks and to the moderation and frugality with which they live that while a Turkish soldier with a handful of dusty rice, some dry meat and fresh water gets along rather well, sorbet is a beverage for the upper classes.

This beverage, that was not at all popular, was taking on aristocratic connotations. And yet here is a description from 1678 taken from *Viaggio alle Indie Orientali* (voyage to the East Indies) by Vincenzo Maria di Santa Caterina from Sienna:

> The public houses, where people gather to drink coffee or black water, sorbets or other similar beverages, like the main streets where the market called Baezzarri is, are covered with arched vaults. There are skylights or windows in the middle with everything stinking and the air suffocating, not only from the crowds of people that fill it but also from the public kitchens where all kinds of meats are cooked for the ordinary people and the poor.

Are we to suppose that, contrary to what Sagredo says, it was a drink of common people? Or was it simply a matter of differences between one city and the next. Only ten years later another diarist offers us another image, a courtly one this time. This comes from *Memorie di viaggi per l'Europa cristiana* (1685) (memoirs of journeys through Christian Europe) by Giovanbattista Pacichelli:

> Companions of the knights, the women were without jewels, and thus exempt from the demands of custom in such situations and they were led by the wrist to the light of crystal lamps, among the music and the iced milk drinks and delicate sorbets (whence came our icecream).

Not all explorers left Italy to discover the rest of the world. Some came from the rest of the world and discovered Italy. This is what happened to Patrick Brydone who wrote *A Voyage to Sicily and Malta* in 1770. On 16 June he wrote:

> We dined together with the bishop, as had been agreed, and we arose from the table convinced that the ancient Grigenti could not have known the true art of banqueting better than their descendants . . . Dessert was all kinds of fruit. The icecreams were even more extravagant, in the shape of peaches, figs, oranges, nuts, etc. and the resemblance to fruit was such that if you were not used to icecream you might easily have been deceived. That is what happened to one good naval officer, at the home of a certain minister of your acquaintance, well known for the elegance of his table and for the rigorousness of the table manners practised in his house. When the second course was finished, they brought, in the guise of rearguard, the icecream, all in the form of fruit and sweets. One of the servants offered the captain what looked like a beautiful peach and he, completely unsuspecting, fully believed it was truly a piece of fruit. Cutting it in two he put a big piece of it in his mouth. At first he only looked worried and puffed out his cheeks to give the mouthful more room, but the freezing stuff quickly got the better of his patience and he began to push it from one side of his mouth to the other, with his eyes watering, until unable to resist any longer he spat it out on his plate, crying, 'Good god! A ball of painted snow!'

To find a poet we must turn back to Italy to Giuseppe

Parini, writing in the eighteenth century. This extraordinary fragment from *Notte* is a truly rococo portrait of icecream. It is the icecream painting that Fragonard never made.

Of ambrosia and of nectar, icecream
gives comfort to your palate and to your soul,
from the land of the gods, it comes.
Look, sir, a gentle being
approaches your lady and, with submissive voice
and clipping his words somewhat,
(in which he resembles his master),
he announces to her
diverse dishes of voluptuous ice.
There, harvested in the snow,
is the sweet strawberry that has betrayed itself
from afar by its very scent,
there is the healthy lemon, there sweet milk;
there, like a great treasure grown amongst us,
is the foreign apple which has usurped the crown
of our own . . .
Arise then and offer to your lady
the taste that delights,
plucked from among the many. Her desires
she will reveal only to you: unwelcome
or unpraised at least the delight arrives,
when for you, her heart does not.
But pay heed to your lady.
Where the still white linen covering her lovely bosom
falls in folds, some ice oozes
unnoticed over the expensive gause
and a pompous bit of fringe threatens in vain
the hopeless spots.

The Frenchman Brillat-Savarin knew that to trace the origins of icecream one needed to go to Italy, as he wrote in his *Physiology of Taste* (1825):

From different places a good-tasting dinner is made, the best things come from France, like the meats from the butcher's shops . . . others from Germany, like sauerkraut . . . and others from Italy, like macaroni, Parmesan, mortadella, polenta and icecream.

A visit to Paris was made by another great Frenchman, the inventor of modern gastronomy, Grimod de La Reynière. Have a look at his 'itinerary' one day to see which were the 'best' addresses for icecream in Paris in those times. We read in the *Itinéraire nutritif* that between the seventeenth and eighteenth centuries the best was the Café du Foi in the Palais Royal 'which every evening after the theatre became the place where the best people, men and women, came to have one of the excellent icecreams'. The café was owned by Madame Lenoir who also owned the Café Corazza. Also mentioned is Monsieur Mazurier in the Champs-Elysées, 'one of the most able icecream makers in Paris'.

And note the tastes and preferences of the seventeenth century, as one Italian writes:

I confess I have always admired Venetian glass, Roman tapestries and mosaics, and the boxes, confectionery and sorbets of Naples and Sicily.

The eighteenth century was a musical century, the time of Bach and Mozart, Vivaldi and Gluck. One of the many forms that was fashionable was the aria. There were all kinds of arias, the aria cantabile, the aria di portamento, the spoken aria, the military aria, the hunting aria, in an endless variety. Among them, one typically found in melodramas, was the 'aria di sorbetto', notable at least as an example of the customs of the day. This aria was usually sung by minor characters in the opera, while the spectators were busily sipping sorbets and icecreams. Though part of the original works, these arias have, thankfully, not survived. The nineteenth-century French novelist Stendhal mentions this particular custom in relation to the Scala:

Often towards the middle of the evening, a servant will come to order the icecreams. There is always some wager pending, and the stakes are always sorbets, which are divine. There are three kinds, icecream, biscuits and little balls. They are really something worth trying. Forever indecisive about which one to choose, I repeat the experience every night.

What about more recent times? Garibaldi in his book *The Thousand* mentions sorbets:

> Of the loafers, I could not discern them, they were hidden in the most unlikely places in their palaces, arranging the hermetic closure of their shutters and eating frozen sorbets, for every other appetite had left them.

A follower of Garibaldi from the same period recalls, in a letter from the recently liberated Palermo:

> We stay in the royal palace and eat servings of icecream as big as beefsteaks.

We can find more testimony to icecream among the nineteenth-century French, with illustrations and almost technical descriptions, as witness this passage from Balzac's *Splendeurs et Misères des Courtisanes*:

> At midnight Esther's ancient dining room had drawn together all the characters in this drama . . . There was no pleasure in that supper at all. Peyrade was a prey to the despair of some invisible worry. Of the young *viveurs* who might have raised the mood of the supper, there were only Lucien and Rastignac. Lucien was feeling very low. Rastignac came after having lost two thousand francs before the supper, and he ate and drank with his mind on recouping his losses afterwards. The three women looked at each other, struck by such coolness. Tedium stripped the food of its flavour. At the end of the meal, icecream called *plombières* was served. Everyone knows this kind of icecream contains small bits of delicate candied fruit sprinkled over the icecream, and comes served in small cups which keep intact the pyramid shape of the icecream. The icecream had been ordered from Madame du Val-Noble in Tortoni whose famous shop was at the corner of rue Taitbout on the main street.

No less famous was a dinner in Flaubert's *Madame Bovary* (1857). Flaubert writes that Emma 'had never seen a pomegranate nor eaten pineapple'. Instead, 'she ate a maraschino cherry icecream that she held with her left hand in a *vermeil* shell, her eyes half closed, the spoon between her teeth'.

And inevitably, at the beginning of this century, there is Proust:

> Icecream (and I truly hope that you do not order me any unless it is in one of those out-of-fashion moulds that come in many different architectural forms) – each time I order some I want temples, churches, obelisks, boulders. What I see first is like a picturesque landscape which then changes from being a monument into cool raspberries or vanilla in my throat.

And in Tolstoy's *War and Peace*, completed in 1868, Natasha when she is a young girl (and for whom I will someday destroy myself from unrequited love) is a glutton for icecream, as we can read in chapter 16 of part one:

> 'Mamma, what sweets are we going to have?' repeated Natasha boldly, with saucy gaiety, confident that her

The itinerant sorbet maker in an eighteenth-century print

prank would not be taken amiss. Sonia and fat little Petya were doubled up with laughter.

'Ice cream, only you will not be allowed any,' said Maria Dmitrievna.

Natasha saw there was nothing to be afraid of and so she braved even Maria Dmitrievna.

'Maria Dmitrievna! What sort of ice cream? I don't like ice cream.'

'Carrot ices.'

'No, what kind, Maria Dmitrievna? What kind?' she almost shrieked. 'I want to know!'

Maria Dmitrievna and the countess burst out laughing, and all the guests joined in. They all laughed, not at Maria Dmitrievna's repartee but at the incredible audacity and smartness of this little girl who had the pluck and wit to tackle Maria Dmitrievna in this fashion.

Natasha only desisted when she was told that there would be pineapple ice.

Icecream on the Screen

We have noted the absence of icecream in paintings. It does exist on posters and billboards but not on canvas. However, as compensation, icecream has played a prominent role in film, as a gastronomic protagonist, and it has had symbolic value as well as being something to eat. Surely the character in *American Graffiti* who eats one icecream after the other for fear that it will melt when his freezer is broken, serves as an introduction to the history of a continent where icecream is a recognized national dish – along with turkey. It is also identified with the Italian-American community among film makers. In films like *The Godfather* or *Raging Bull*, the characters are always eating pizza, spaghetti and icecream. These are two of the most typical symbolic uses of icecream in film. The third is one which links it by a fine, almost invisible thread to comedies about vacations and recently to eroticism in the soft-porn of some French and Italian films. In silent films, Laurel and Hardy substituted icecream for custard pie, the Marx Brothers used icecream in *Monkey Business*, Charlie Chaplin let an icecream melt on the bosom of a lady, and Jacques Tati used it in *Monsieur Hulot*.

Here ends my rapid and surely incomplete look at ice-cream, a simple pleasure with a long history, a world of varieties and myriad tempting flavours, created in the Mediterranean for the rich and now enjoyed by everyone all over the world.

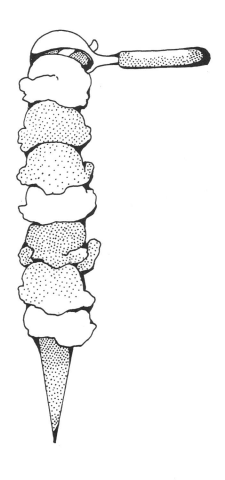